COUNTRY STUDIES

CW01574541

CHINA

... book is to be
the last da...

Trevor Higginbottom
Tony White
Series Editor: John Hopkin

Heinemann

R10199
19 SEP 2000

For more information about Heinemann Library books, or to order, please telephone +44 (0)1865 888066, or send a fax to +44 (0)1865 314091.
You can visit our web site at *www.heinemann.co.uk*

Heinemann Educational Publishers
Halley Court, Jordan Hill, Oxford, OX2 8EJ
A division of Reed Educational & Professional Publishing Ltd
Heinemann is a registered trademark of Reed Educational & Professional Publishing Ltd

OXFORD MELBOURNE AUCKLAND
JOHANNESBURG BLANTYRE GABORONE
IBADAN PORTSMOUTH NH (USA) CHICAGO

© Trevor Higginbottom and Tony White, 1999

Copyright notice
All rights reserved. No part of this publication may be reproduced in any material form (including photocopying or storing it in any medium by electronic means and whether or not transiently or incidentally to some other use of this publication) without the prior written permission of the copyright owner, except in accordance with the provisions of the Copyright, Designs and Patents Act 1988 or under the terms of a licence issued by the Copyright Licensing Agency Ltd, 90 Tottenham Court Road, London W1P 0LP. Applications for the copyright owner's written permission to reproduce any part of this publication should be addressed to the publisher.

First published 1999

ISBN 0 431 01417 5 (hardback)

ISBN 0 431 01418 3 (paperback)

British Library Cataloguing in Publication Data

Higginbottom, Trevor
China. – (Country studies)
1. China – Social conditions – 1949 – Juvenile literature
2. China – History – 1949 – Juvenile literature
3. China – Description and travel – Juvenile literature
I. Title II. White, Tony
951'.059
ISBN 0 431 01417 5

03 02 01 00
10 9 8 7 6 5 4 3 2 1

Typeset and illustrated by Hardlines, Charlbury, Oxford OX7 3PS

Originated by Ambassador Litho, Bristol BS16 3HH

Printed and bound in Spain by Edelvives

Acknowledgements
The authors wish to thank Associate Professor George Lin, University of Hong Kong, for his advice and support in writing this book.

The publishers would like to thank the following for permission to reproduce copyright material.

Maps and extracts
p.4 John Bryan Starr, Understanding China / Profile Books, London 1997, 1999; **p.6 C** Fang Jun Yi, An Outline of China's Geography / Era Book Company Limited, Hong Kong, 1980; **p.11 D** Mike Senior, Trends in Geography 2 / Pearson Education, Hong Kong; **p.16 A** Robert Prosser, Places and Cases: The World / Stanley Thornes Publishers Limited, Cheltenham; **p.17 B** Professional Geographer 48(1) / Blackwell Publishers, Boston, USA, 1996; **p.17 A** South China Morning Post; **p.18** South China Morning Post; **p.20** Butterworth Heinemann Asia; **p.27 A** Associated Press, New York; **p.32** South China Morning Post; **p.33** South China Morning Post; **p.35 C** Brookes, Clammer, Currie, Higginbottom et al, Geography Today / Collins Educational, London; **p.35** top South China Morning Post; **p.44** China Today / The China Welfare Institute, Beijing, 1999; **p.50** Paul Theroux, Going to See the Dragon / Harper's Magazine, 1993, New York; **p.56 A** South China Morning Post; **p.56 B** South China Morning Post; **p.57 C** Sunday Standard, Hong Kong, 1993; **p.58 B** © The Economist, London (1 May 1999); **p.59 C** South China Morning Post.

Photographs
Cover photos: Shanghai street scene: Tony Stone Images; Chinese girl: The Image Bank.
p. 4 B Getty Images; **p. 6 A** APL; **p. 6 B** Getty Images; **p. 6 D** China Photo Library; **p. 7 E** Tony Stone; **p. 9 C** APL; **p. 10 A** South China Morning Post Picture Library; **p. 10 B** Soug office; **p. 23 D** Getty Images; **p. 24 A** Eye Ubiquitous; **p. 26 A** South China Morning Post Picture Library; **p. 29 D** Eye Ubiquitous; **p. 30 C** South China Morning Post Picture Library; **p. 32 A** Getty Images; **p. 39 E** South China Morning Post Picture Library; **p. 40 D** Getty Images; **p. 41 E** China Photo Librath China Morning Post Picture Library; **p. 13 C** Getty Images; **p. 14** Chinese Government; **p. 15 B** South China Morning Post Picture Library; **p. 17 D** South China Morning Post Picture Library; **p. 19 C** Hong Kong survey and mapping office; **p. 19 D** Hong Kong survey and mapping office; **p. 20 A** Getty Images; **p. 22** A Hong Kong Survey and mappinry; **p. 43 D(i)** Getty Images; **p. 43 D(ii)** Getty Images; **p. 43 D(iii)** China Photo Library; **p. 45 A** Stock House Ltd; **p. 46 B** Trevor Higginbottom; **p. 48 A** APL; **p. 48 B** South China Morning Post Picture Library; **p. 50 C** China Photo Library **p. 52 A** APL; **p. 56 D(i)** Xinhua Picture Agency, **(ii)** Agence France-Presse **p. 59 E** South China Morning Post Picture Library

The publishers have made every effort to trace the copyright holders, but if they have inadvertently overlooked any, they will be pleased to make the necessary arrangements at the first opportunity.

Any words appearing in bold, **like this**, are explained in the Glossary

Contents

THOMAS ADAMS
SCHOOL LIBRARY

1 INTRODUCING CHINA

An emerging giant

▶ Why is China such an important country for us to study?

China is home to almost a quarter of the world's population. Within the next few decades the country could become a global economic and political **superpower**. The growth of China will, almost certainly, have a great impact on the world in the early part of the twenty-first century.

In the last ten years there has been a great deal of investment in China by foreign countries and firms. The country itself is investing abroad. This had led to changing lifestyles for individuals.

A China in the world, 1996

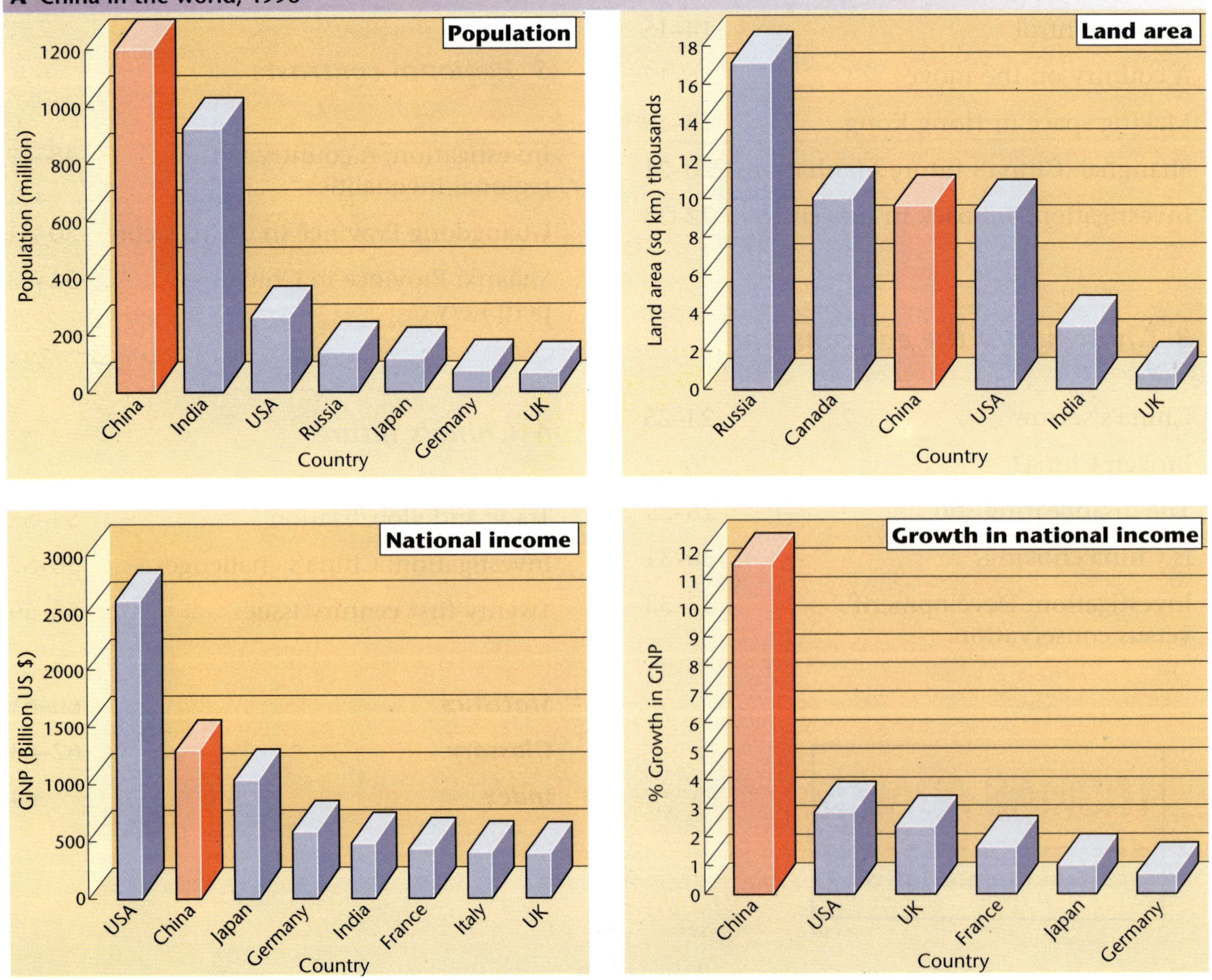

"There has been a great deal of good news coming out of China in recent years:

- China has one of the world's fastest growing economies. Indeed, there are those who predict that, at its current rate of growth, China's will be the world's largest economy by 2040, surpassing those of Japan and of the United States.
- Economic growth has greatly improved the standard of living for most, if not all, Chinese people. Rural incomes are three times what they were in 1978, the beginning of the current period of economic reform, and urban incomes are up nearly five times.
- There has also been some relaxation of the tight control the Chinese government maintained over its population. Most of the Chinese people are enjoying much more freedom from government interference in their lives than they did fifteen years ago."

Understanding China, John Bryan Starr, 1998

B Administrative regions and main cities of China

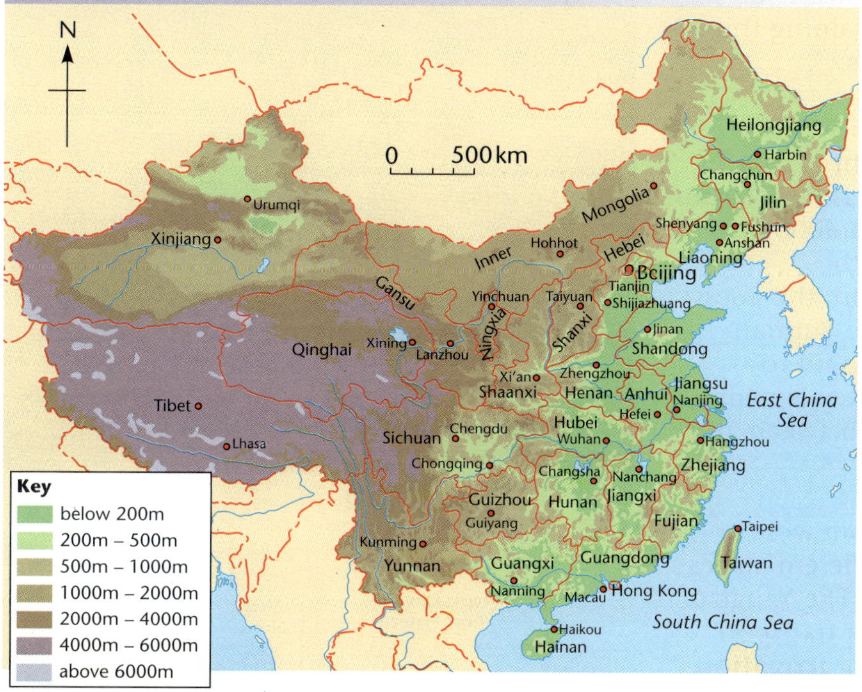

C McDonald's in Beijing

FACT FILE

Foreign investment in China, 1996

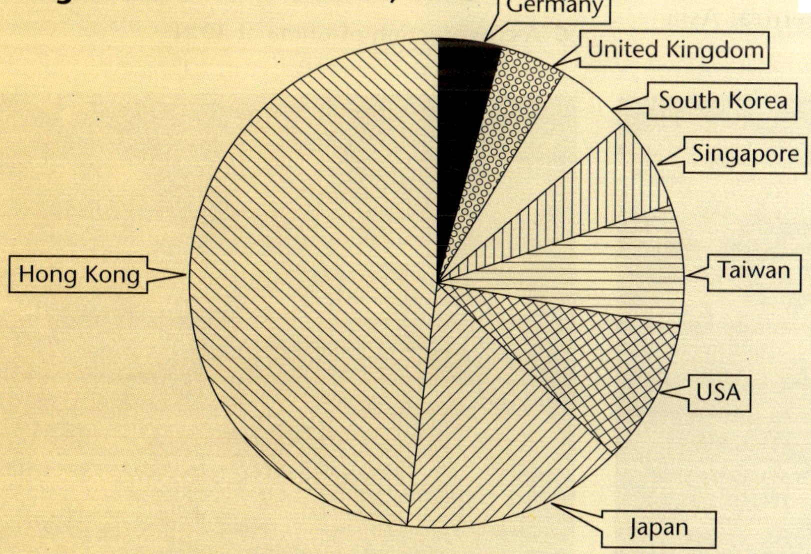

China's physical landscapes

- ▶ What are the main physical regions of China?
- ▶ What types of landscapes do they contain?

China can be divided into a number of physical regions, each with a distinctive landscape. Two thirds of the country's total area consists of mountains and **plateaux**. The remaining third is an area of river basins and plains.

As shown in cross-section C, the physical geography of China can be thought of as a series of three steps. The first step is the Plateau of Tibet, with an average height of 4000 metres. The second step includes the Mongolian Plateau, the Tarim Basin, the Loess Plateau, the Sichuan Basin and the Yunnan-Guizhou Plateau, all of which descend to heights of 900 metres. The third step is mainly an area of **river plains** at heights between 700 and 800 metres.

China's two longest rivers flow from west to east across these three steps, at different stages in gorges, basins and floodplains. The Yangtze River, 6380km in length, is a main transport route and a rich source of water for **irrigation** and hydro-electric power. The Yellow River, 5465km in length, gets its name from the load of sediment it picks up as it crosses the **Loess** Plateau, which is covered by great thicknesses of wind-borne dust blown from central Asia (see pages 28 and 29).

B The Tibetan Plateau

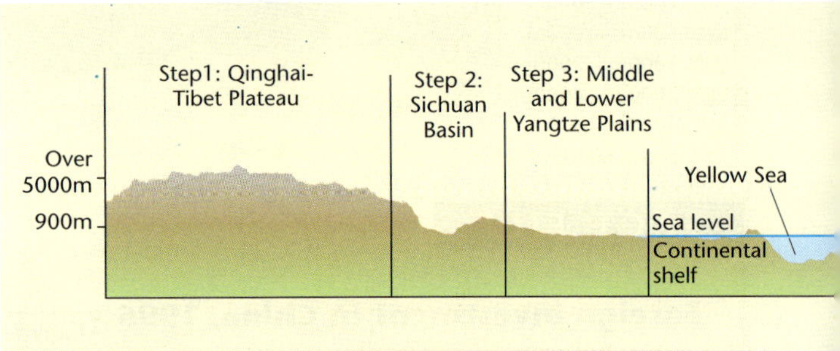

C A cross-section of China at 30°N

A The Sichuan Basin

D The Yangtze Plain

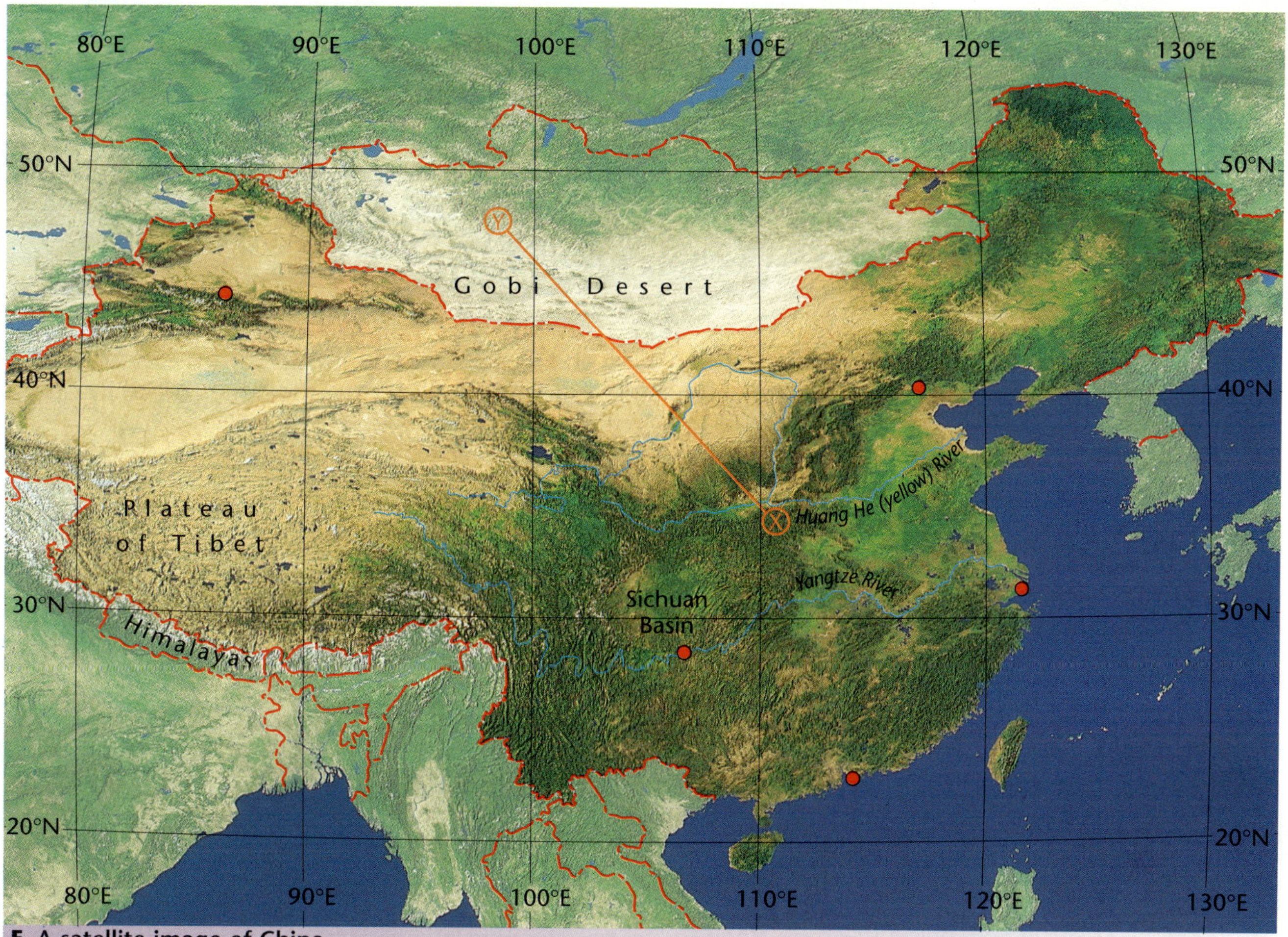

E A satellite image of China

FACT FILE

Natural resources

40% of China's cultivated land is located in the North China Plain. The country has the largest hydro-electric power potential in the world. 70% of this is distributed in four south-western provinces and Tibet.

China leads the world in its reserves of tungsten, molybdenum, vanadium and titanium. It also has vast reserves of coal, iron ore, copper, silver, tin, nickel and asbestos.

Main types of land use in China: 1987

Land use	%
Cultivated land	10.3
Fruit, tea, mulberry and rubber plantations	0.3
Forestry	12.7
Grass lands	29.8
Urban and industrial areas and transport routes	8.5
Inland waterways and shallow seas	3.1
Stone bare ground, deserts, marshes, permanent frozen lands and glaciers	19.4

China's contrasting climates

- How and why does the climate vary across China?
- How does the climate affect people's lives?

Similarities and differences of climate

Much of inland China has a **continental climate**, with extremely cold, dry winters and hot, wetter summers. However, China is a very large country so the climate varies enormously from place to place (**A**). Some of the main factors to influence China's climate are:

- the south is hotter because the sun is at a higher angle in the sky, so it heats the ground more intensely;
- the west is mostly mountainous and it gets colder at higher altitudes due to the lower air pressure;
- the coast is wetter since air blowing from the sea tends to pick up more moisture than air blowing from the land;
- the south is also wetter because warmer air can hold more moisture;
- winds blowing from the north of China bring colder air than winds from the south.

		Jan	Feb	Mar	Apr	May	Jun	Jul	Aug	Sep	Oct	Nov	Dec
Beijing	Precipitation (mm)	4	5	8	17	35	78	243	141	58	16	11	3
	Temperature °C	–5	2	5	14	20	25	26	25	20	13	4	-3

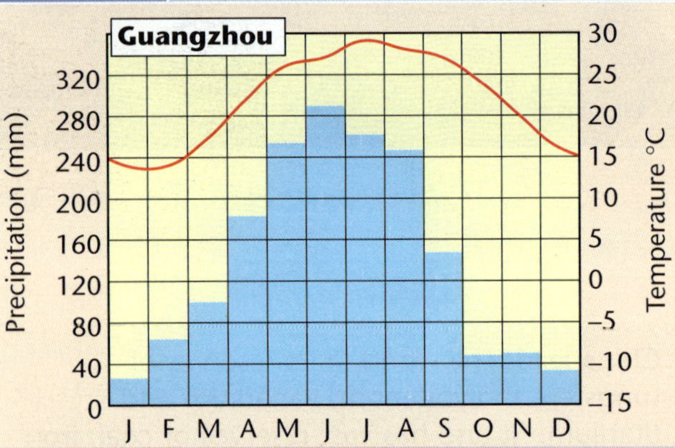

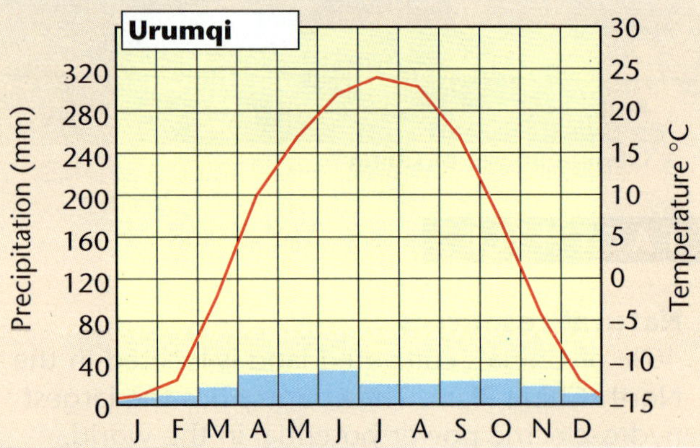

A Climatic contrasts in China

How air masses affect the seasons

Air masses are large areas of the atmosphere where the temperature and humidity of the air is fairly uniform. The air masses get these characteristics from the area where they form and they change as they move away from this source area. Diagram **B** shows the usual situation in the winter.

In summer, the winter pattern is reversed. The land mass heats up and air rises to create low pressure (a depression) over the north. This draws air in from the warm seas to the south and east. Summer is warmer and wetter, particularly in the south. The hot summer days here lead to rapid **convectional uplift** of hot air, and result in frequent, violent thunderstorms.

How climate affects the people

The climate has a huge impact on many aspects of people's lives wherever they live. Farming is obviously affected by the climate, but so are features like building design, communications, energy supply and demand, leisure activities, and many other aspects of our way of life. Every year thousands of Chinese are killed by extreme weather events such as floods, blizzards, typhoons, hailstorms and droughts. Recent examples include:

- 50 killed by a powerful sand storm in Xinjiang;

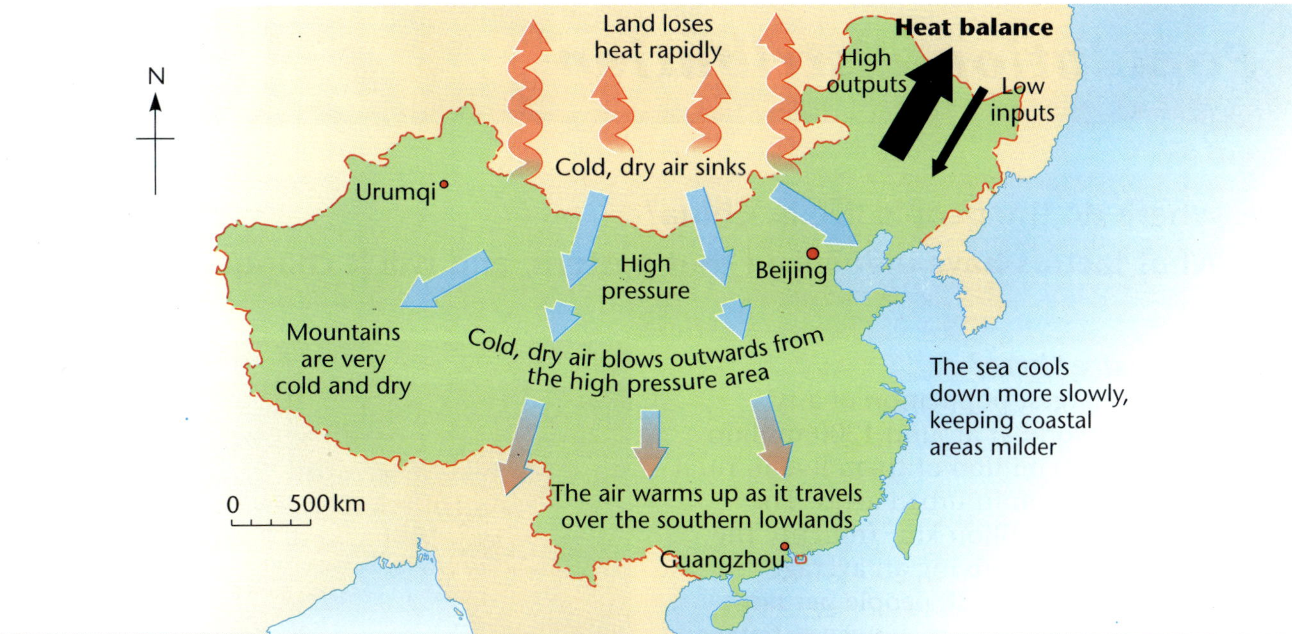

B Effects of the anticyclone over northern China in winter

- hailstones up to 8cm in diameter in Hunan killed 9 people and destroyed crops;
- 600 killed in traffic accidents after snowstorms in Beijing;
- 103 000 trapped by snow in remote Xinjiang Mountains;
- 14 killed and 42 injured when lightning hit a building in Guizhou province;
- 1 200 killed in flooding of the Yangtze River.

C Snow over the Imperial Palace, Beijing

FACT FILE

Monsoons, typhoons and snowstorms

Much of south-east Asia has what is described as a monsoon climate. Although it is frequently used to describe a sudden wet season, the term monsoon is derived from the Arabic word *mawsim* meaning seasonal wind. The winter monsoon brings cold and very dry air from the north. The summer monsoon brings warm, moist air from the south. Droughts and floods occur as a result of abnormal monsoons, such as in 1954 when a mass of cold air from the north blocked the passage of the summer monsoon and caused it to bring torrential rain and widespread flooding to the Yangtze valley.

Typhoons frequently form in the warm waters of the western Pacific Ocean and travel westwards towards Asia. Although the more exposed islands of the Philippines frequently get the worst battering, the coast of China is still likely to be hit by around five typhoons a year. In September 1996, Typhoon Sally made landfall in the coastal province of Guangdong. The death toll was put at 147, with more than 5 000 injured, 272 000 houses destroyed and 1 220 000 damaged. 15 million people as well as 680 000 hectares of crops were affected. Highways, telecommunication facilities, dykes and dams suffered severe damage.

In January 1997 the north-west of China suffered the most severe snowstorm for 30 years. Temperatures fell to -36°C and over 2 metres of snow covered the area. 320 000 people were cut off from the rest of the country and at least 36 people died as a result of the storms.

Population distribution

▶ Where do the people live in China?
▶ What factors have influenced that pattern, and will it change?

How many are there?

China has the largest population of any country in the world at around 1200 million people. About 900 million of them live in rural areas and 300 million in urban areas. The country covers 9.6 million km^2 (roughly the same size as the USA), giving an average **population density** of 130 people per km^2. Some regions of the country, however, have a far higher population density than others.

A A high density location

B A low density location

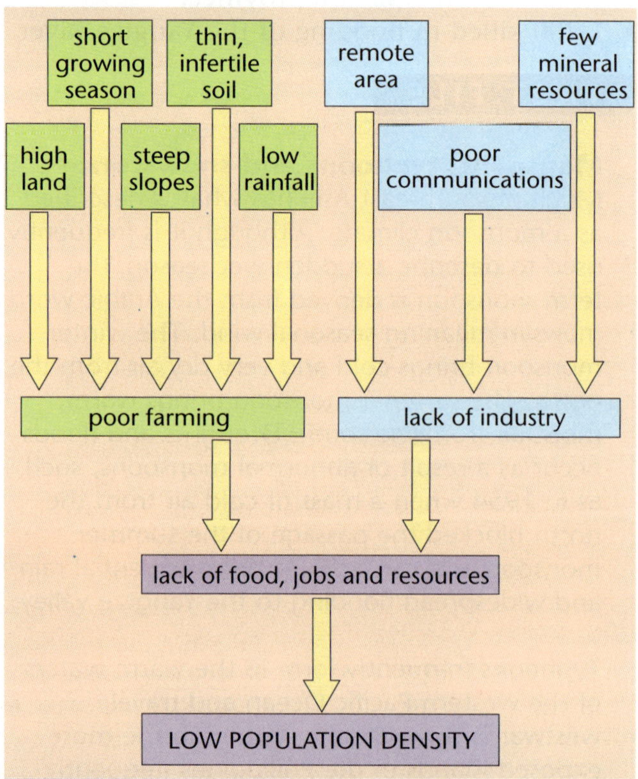

C Reasons for a low population density

Low density regions

The western part of China has about 10% of the population living in 60% of the land area. Some areas have fewer than 1 person per km^2. Some of the reasons for the low population density are shown in diagram **C**.

High density regions

The highest population densities have always been found in the eastern lowlands. Here the floodplains have fertile soils and longer **growing seasons**. Even in the drier areas the rivers can often be used to irrigate farmland.

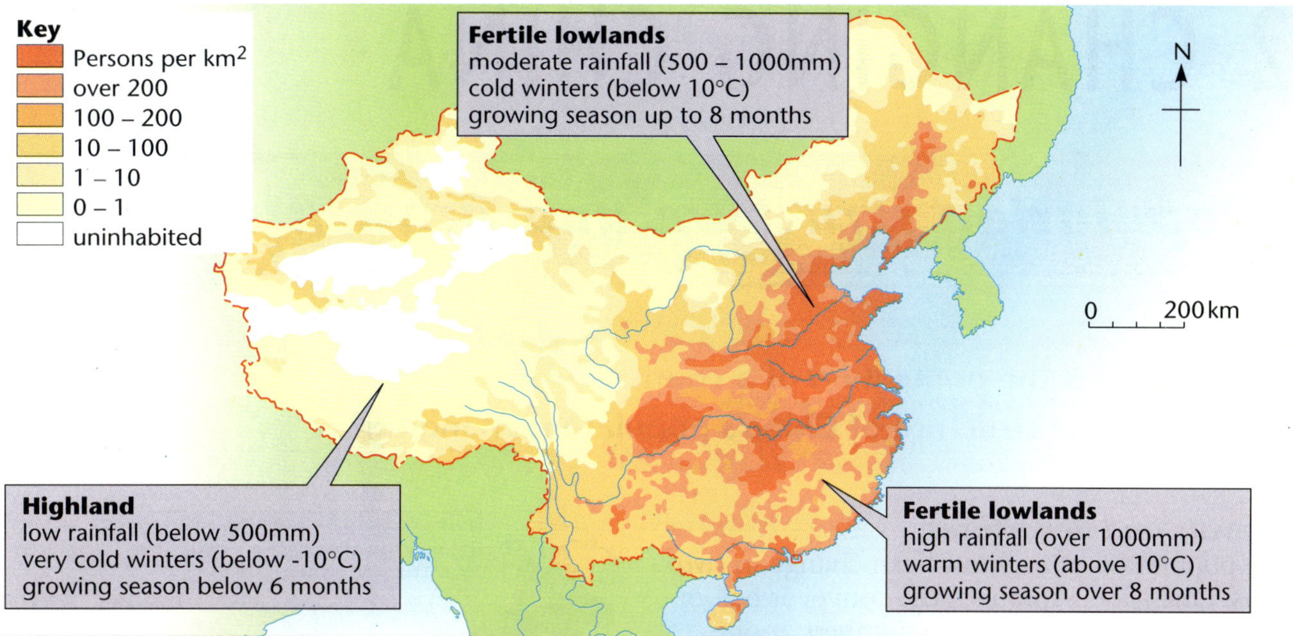

D Population density of China

Administrative and commercial cities are found throughout China. Most of the industrial cities of China are in the north-east where important mineral resources, such as iron ore, coal and oil, are found. Industries such as iron and steel, chemicals, motorcars and textiles have developed using these raw materials and energy.

The **accessibility** of the eastern region is another reason for its higher population density. Trade by ship has led to the growth of many large ports like Tianjin, Qingdao, Shanghai and Hong Kong along the coast of China. There are also more railways, roads and inland waterways in the east of the country.

Government influence

In the 1950s many people moved from the crowded cities to remote rural areas. Until recently each person was registered in one place and was not allowed to move elsewhere without permission. This system has now been relaxed and there are thought to be about 100 million '**floating workers**' who have moved from the countryside to the cities to look for work. Unless the government makes rural life more attractive, the pattern of **population distribution** may become more uneven in the future.

FACT FILE

The spread of the Chinese people

People first began to settle in the north-eastern part of present-day China about 8 000 years ago. They chose the valleys of three major rivers, the Yellow River, the Wei and the Yangtze, where the soils of the flood plains were fertile and there was an adequate supply of water. The Chinese state now contains a variety of ethnic groups.

Over 90% of the population consider themselves to be Han Chinese and the remainder of the population is made up of 55 'minority nationalities', such as the Zhuang, Tibetans and Mongolians, with their own languages. Many people believe that the reason the different linguistic groups did not become separate states, as in Europe, was because of a common written language.

The minority nationalities are found predominantly in the west of the country, in the least hospitable areas and the population density averages about 8 people per km^2. On the lowland eastern half of the country the population density averages over 300 people per km^2, rising to more than 600 per km^2 on the plains.

Obtaining reliable figures is not easy. For the 1981 census over six million census officers were needed, but the figures for some areas may still not be accurate.

2 CHANGING CHINA

Population structure and growth

▶ How does the population of a country grow?
▶ How is the structure of China's population changing?

Arrivals and departures

The population of a country can change in two ways. One way is through 'the conveyor belt of life', where births add to the numbers at one end and deaths remove people at the other. By subtracting the number of deaths from the number of births you can calculate the rate of natural increase of population in the country. The other way that the population may change is by people leaping off and on the conveyor belt to and from other countries. These movements are called **international migration**.

China's growth spurt

China's population has grown very slowly for most of its history. Although the **birth rate** was high, so was the **death rate**. Even as recently as 1950 people's **life expectancy** in China was only 40 years.

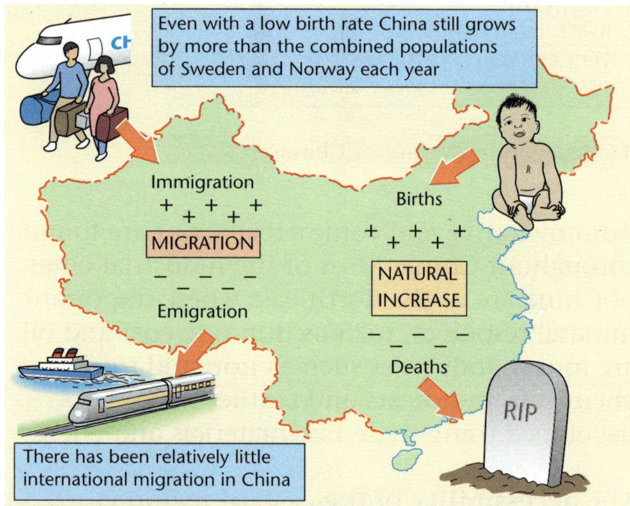

A How the population changes

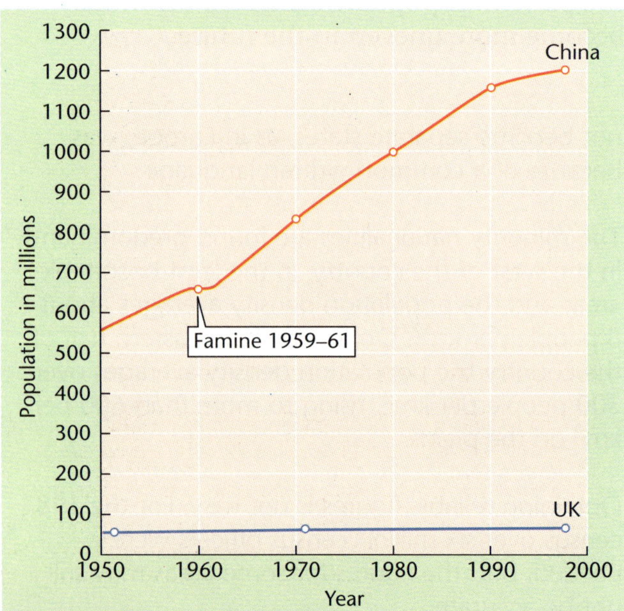

B Population growth in China, 1950–98

It took around a thousand years for China's population to double from 50 million to 100 million. It took only forty years for it to double from 500 million to 1 000 million. After the Communists gained power in 1949 they encouraged population growth. As living conditions improved and the **death rate** fell, the population began to grow alarmingly and by the 1960s the authorities were encouraging birth control.

Population pyramids

A population pyramid is a useful diagram to show how the population is divided among males and females of different ages. The shape of the pyramid can tell what is happening to the population. High percentages at the bottom of the pyramid show a high birth rate. A rapid narrowing of the shape towards the top means a high death rate in the country. A war, famine or mass emigration will show up as a 'dent' in the shape of the pyramid.

China's 'greying' population

China's birth and death rates have fallen and the life expectancy has risen. This means that the proportion of older people in the country is rising. Many countries are worried about the effect that this might have on their economy. The elderly are often seen as a drain on resources, although the main problem may be that these countries have not made plans for the changing age structure of their population.

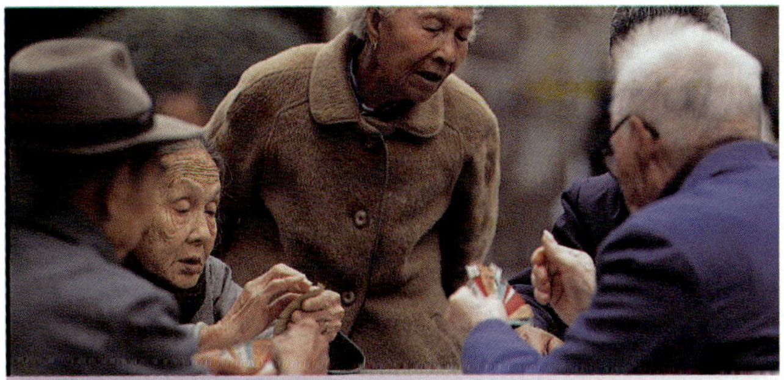

C Elderly card players in Fujian

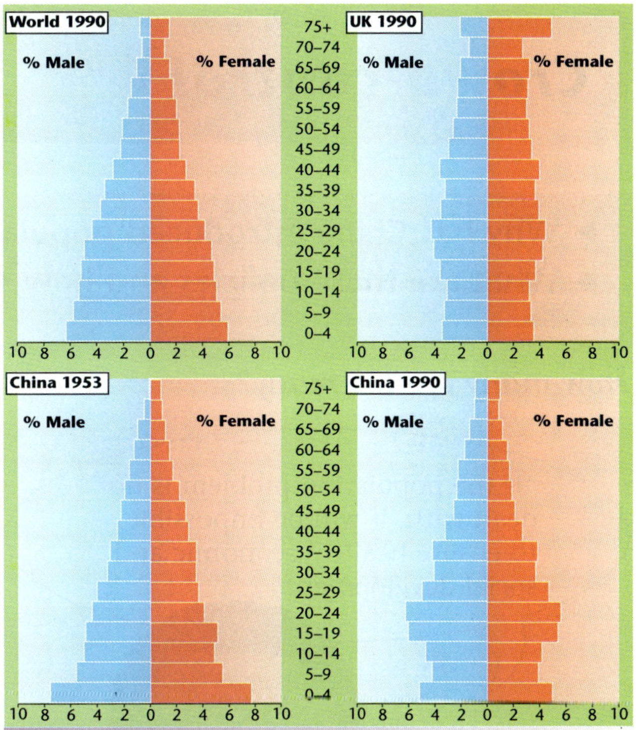

D Population pyramids compared

FACT FILE

An asset or a hindrance?

China's large population has been seen as both an asset and a hindrance by different people in the past. A writer in the third century BC said of China that "an increasing population over a long period of time would bring about strife and disaster." Sun Yat-Sen, the leader of the country early in the twentieth century, wrote that "at present China is already suffering from over-population which will bring impending danger in its wake.... In time of great drought and famine, many people will starve to death."

However, Mao Zedong, the country's first communist leader, saw the large population as its main asset. Each person was seen as an extra pair of hands to help defend and develop the country.

In the 1950s and 60s the birth rate was well above 30 per thousand per year. In the 1970s Premier Zhou Enlai believed that controlling population growth was necessary for economic development in the country. His aim was to reduce the birth rate to 20 per thousand per year by 1980 with a policy referred to as 'late, spacing and few'. Couples were encouraged to marry late, leave four years between children, and restrict their children to two.

The present aim of the Chinese government is to reduce the birth rate to 13 per thousand. The policy today allows for only one child per family. The impact of this policy is discussed on page 14.

Life expectancy 1930–1997

Year	1930	1950	1970	1997
Life expectancy	24	40	63	70

Population changes 1950–1997

Year	Birth rate (per 1000)	Death rate (per 1000)	Natural increase (per 1000)
1950	44	25	19
1970	31	9	22
1990	18	7	11
1997	17	7	10

Crowd control

- ▶ Why has China introduced population policies?
- ▶ What are these policies and how successful have they been?

How many are too many?

"If the population problem is not dealt with, it will be impossible to ensure healthy economic and social development"

Zou Jiahua, Vice-Premier.

The number of people living in an area is usually related to the resources that are available there. People have basic needs, such as food, water and shelter, which they get from the environment. Some environments are rich in resources and will support many people, while others will support very few.

Population policies

In the 1970s couples were encouraged to marry later, to leave at least four years between births and to have only two children. This was replaced by a one-child policy in the 1980s. The aim was for zero population growth – a balance of births and deaths – by the year 2040. The policy is not a law, but there are incentives for parents who follow the aim and penalties for those who do not.

Rural and urban differences

In the rural areas the policy was strongly opposed and couples were allowed to have a second child if the first was a girl. Traditionally, boys have been valued more highly than girls since they keep the family name while girls join another family through marriage. Cases of female **infanticide** have been reported and

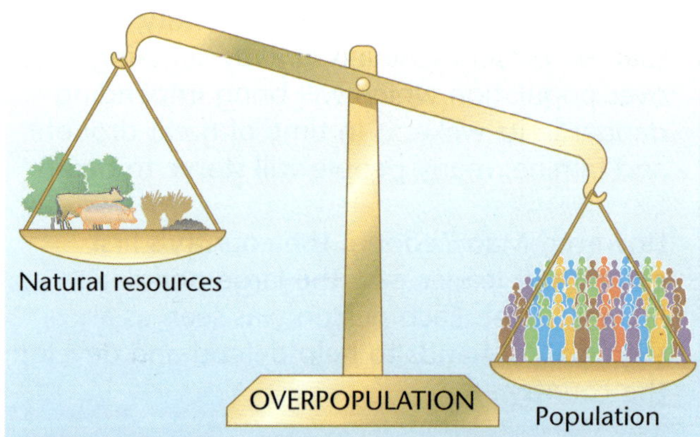

A A population imbalance

Incentives for one-child families:
- financial rewards
- free schooling
- free medical provision
- government jobs, housing and pensions.

Penalties for second pregnancies:
- fines (often a year's salary)
- no more free schooling nor medical care
- pressure to undergo abortions or sterilisations
- loss of government jobs, housing and pensions.

many births are simply not recorded. Tests to determine the sex of unborn babies are now officially banned.

The policy has been more widely accepted in urban areas where people are less traditional. City populations are more educated than those in the countryside and women are more likely to follow careers. Space is limited and an extra child has a greater influence on the family's standard of living.

Success or failure?

"China's efforts to control population growth proved to be successful, with a population 200 million less than what it could have been had nothing been done," according to the Chinese government.

A typical family now has four grandparents and two parents devoting all their attention to one child (referred to as the 4-2-1 system). These children, easily spoiled and increasingly overweight, are called "little emperors and empresses". There has been a rise in juvenile misbehaviour, crime and violence recently and many blame the change in family structure for making the young Chinese expect more attention and success.

B A "little emperor"

FACT FILE

Unforeseen consequences

There are many possible unforeseen consequences when governments try to control the natural growth of population. In China, two of these consequences have been a huge gender imbalance and the reduction of the traditional source of care for the elderly.

There are, on average around the world, 106 boys born for every 100 girls. In China, in 1995, there were 118 boys under the age of 5 for every 100 girls. This has resulted in an estimated 90 million bachelors unable to find wives, and the imbalance will increase in the future. Kidnappings of women and the sale of brides is not uncommon in some areas. It is estimated that 64 000 women have been rescued from forced marriages since 1990.

A second problem has been caring for the increasing percentage of elderly people. In the sixth century the Chinese philosopher Confucius stated that "any child's duty is to take care of their parents' livelihood".

With the one child system, that child could be responsible for the welfare of four grandparents. State industries paid their employees pensions in the past, but recent reforms, resulting in millions of lay-offs, will make this impossible in the future. In 1995, the Chinese leadership began taking steps to establish a nationwide pension system. The government even passed a law in 1996 to penalise those offspring who refuse to provide support for their parents. As the population of pensioners begins to exceed that of workers in many regions, the problem will only get worse.

A country on the move

▶ What is the pattern of migration within China?
▶ Why do people move? How does this change affect their lives?

A large number of people are moving within China. In 1995, at least 100 million people were living in a different province from the one in which they were born. This migration has occurred mainly since 1984, when the communist government began to allow people to move more freely. At least four out of every ten migrants have moved from rural to urban areas.

Push factors
In the rural areas:
- the amount of agricultural land is decreasing;
- farming is being modernised;
- there are few job opportunities.

Therefore many people are without land, jobs or income.

Pull factors
In the urban areas:
- there are many new construction, manufacturing and service industries;
- more jobs are created;
- higher wages are available;
- there is more housing.

Therefore there is a growing demand for workers.

Map **A** shows which of China's provinces have gained and lost population because of internal migration. The population of many of the provinces of eastern China has increased rapidly because the government has encouraged industries in **Special Economic Zones**. For example, as a result more than a million **migrants** were attracted to Guangdong Province between 1985 and 1990 (Map **D**). Zhuhai was one of China's five Special Economic Zones set up in the early 1980s (Extract **C**).

A Population change caused by internal migration, 1985–90

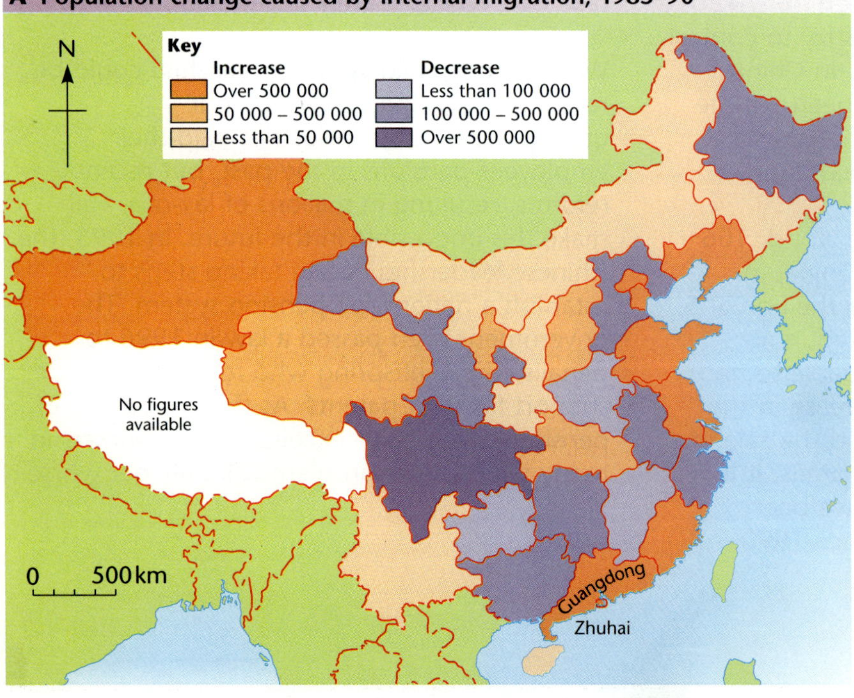

B Migrant women in Zhuhai

Migrants flock to Zhuhai

In the harsh midday sun, Zhuhai's Jida industrial estate is a cheerless concrete expanse with row upon row of factories. But come dusk, it is transformed into a lively meeting place as vendors hawk their wares and migrant women stream out of factories to pick up their dinner. Conversations float through the air, some in Putonghua, most in dialects from nothern China.

Almost half of Zhuhai's population of 607 000 are migrant workers, and 80 per cent of them are women aged 16 to 25.

The economic zone has a special lure for these women, many of whom move there to escape the bleak work prospects back home. Especially at a time when massive layoffs are taking place at state-owned companies throughout the mainland, Zhuhai is viewed as a land of opportunity.

Tan Shen, a senior researcher at the Chinese Academy of Social Science, estimates there are four million migrant women concentrated in the Guandong boomtowns of Dongguan, Zhongshan, Shunde, Shenzhen and Zhuhai. She says the economic success of these cities is largely due to the female migrant labour force.

"These girls who work in joint-venture factories, restaurants or hair salons, as servants of hawkers, are mostly from Sichuan, Hunan, Guangxi and Jiangxi," says Ms Tan, adding that the northern provinces, whose economies developed later than those in the south, have surplus labour.

While many in the north can make money only during the harvest, in Zhuhai they have a steady income.

"Once they've worked in the south for three or four years, the cleverer ones will go back with their savings and start a village enterprise," says Wang Xiulin, editor of China Women's News. "They can be hair stylists or open a clothing shop."

But not everything is as rosy as is it seems.

"The girls may have adjustment problems when they come to the big cities. They work long hours and have little social life.'

Extract from *South China Morning Post*, 29 March 1998

C Zhuhai province: push and pull

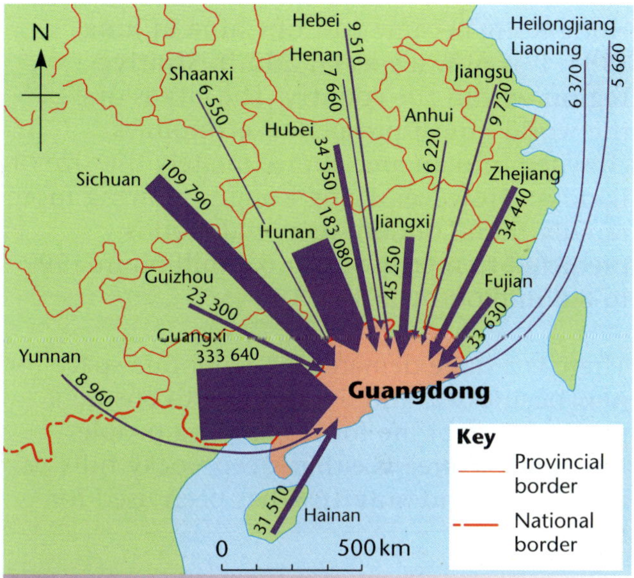

D Migration to Guangdong from other parts of China, 1985–90

FACT FILE

The migrant population

The five Chinese cities attracting the most migrants in 1996 were Beijing (3.5 million), Shanghai (3.5 million), Guangzhou (1.8 million), Wuhan (1.5 million) and Chengdu 800 000. During the Lunar New Year holidays in February 1996, it was estimated that 90 million migrants travelled home by various modes of transport.

The Chinese Government is concerned that many migrants do not observe the country's single child family planning policy. However, officials acknowledge that it is impossible to estimate the number of children in the moving population.

In 1997, the Beijing Public Security Bureau estimated that 56% of the crimes reported in the capital were carried out by migrants.

Beijing is trying to house migrant workers in five new suburban districts. It is hoped that this will help to reduce social problems. However, some permanent residents are concerned that these new districts will attract even more migrants to the city.

Making space in Hong Kong

- ▶ Why does Hong Kong need more economic and living space?
- ▶ What are the advantages and disadvantages of land reclamation?

Hong Kong became part of China in June, 1997. It is now a **special administrative region** within the country. The city is one of the world's most prosperous economies crowded into an area approximately the size of London. However, Hong Kong is growing more rapidly than London. Its population is predicted to increase from 6.7 million in 1999 to 8.2 million by 2016.

There is a huge demand for economic space for new businesses, and living space to ensure a good quality of life for Hong Kong people. Much of the area is either steep, rocky hills or marshland, and only 16% has been used for building on.

One solution has been to create very high density for business and housing. Another has been land reclamation. Since 1945 almost 6000 hectares of land has been developed by this means.

An example of land reclamation has been the infilling of Victoria Harbour which is surrounded by Hong Kong's central business district. The proposal to build Kai Tak City would reduce the size of Victoria Harbour even further. As with many other major urban planning schemes, the proposal is receiving much opposition.

A Extract from the *South China Morning Post*

Plan for Kai Tak City unveiled

4 September, 1998

A $36 billion plan to build a "city within a city" at the former Kai Tak airport site was unveiled yesterday.

Housing for 320 000 people, 90 000 permanent jobs and the SAR's largest urban park will be created on the 579-hectare site, more than half of which is to be reclaimed from the harbour. The four-stage development will take 18 years to complete and will see the building of 118 000 flats with roads, shops, government and school buildings, a hospital, godowns and recreational areas.

The 50-hectare Metropolitan Park is intended not just for new residents and people living in Kwun Tong and To Kwa Wan who do not have enough open space, but for people from throughout Hong Kong and international visitors.

There will also be a waterfront promenade running the length of the development, an international-standard sports stadium, a transport museum and an aviation "academy" to mark Kai Tak's past, as well as two new trunk roads and a possible railway line. Some industrial areas bordering the site will be rezoned as residential to improve the area.

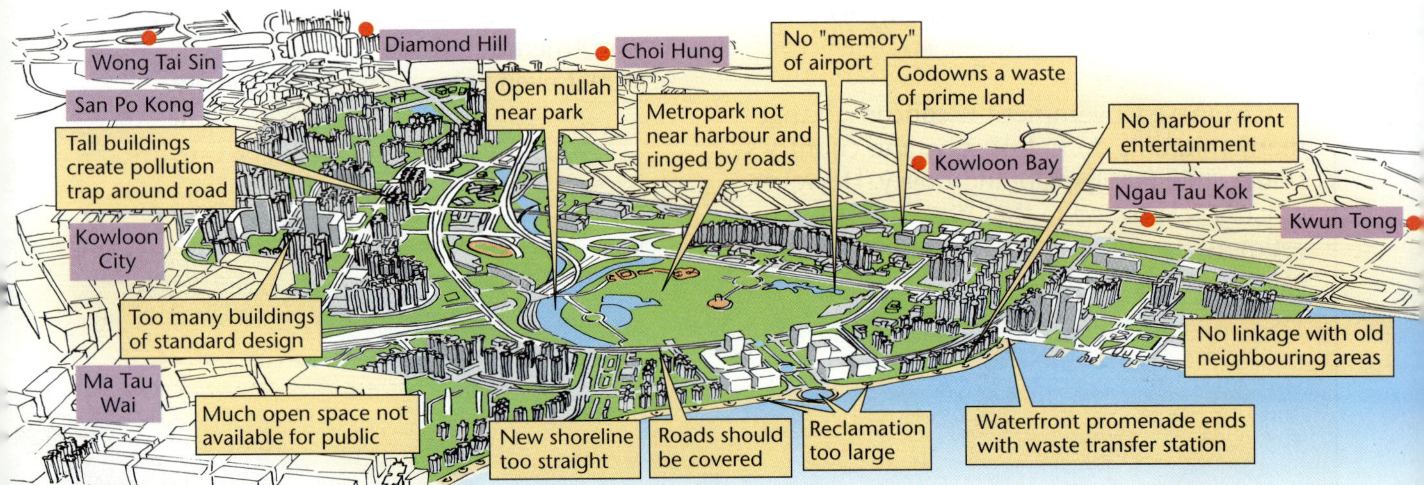

B Design for Kai Tak City in 2016: what the critics say

from the *South China Morning*

C Victoria Harbour, 1964

D Victoria Harbour, 1997

E Some views of the supporters of further reclamation in Victoria Harbour

- Reclamation can provide 'natural' growth of nearby urbanised areas. Existing service and transport networks can be extended.
- These types of schemes can be completed quite quickly.
- Publicly owned land is created.
- In these central areas the value of this land is high.
- When the infill is taking place it creates a site for public dumping.
- Reclamation schemes can get rid of polluted areas of confined water like the Kowloon Bay **Nullah**.

F Some views of the opponents of further reclamation in Victoria Harbour

- There will be less water, more buildings and therefore more people; this will increase water pollution.
- Victoria Harbour is being spoilt as a world famous tourist attraction.
- The dredging carried out during reclamation causes sediment to be suspended in the water. This affects the Harbour's ecosystem.
- There will be an increase in road traffic in these already congested coastal areas.
- As this busy Harbour gets narrower, it will become more dangerous for shipping.
- Heavy vehicles carrying infill material will cause traffic and environmental problems.

FACT FILE

Views on the Kai Tak City scheme

The District Planning Officer for Kowloon, Lau Sing, said: "We don't want to see just a pile of houses along the waterfront. We want to see some landscaped corridors. The 'metro park' will be a green lung for the area".

Michael Choi Ngai-miu, Managing Director of Hong Kong Property, said the plan would benefit the property and retail markets in the area.

When the Director of Planning Peter Pun Kwok-Shing announced the new Kai Tak scheme he said: "It will have a very important influence on Hong Kong's development in the 21st-century. It will be a city within a city."

Lisa Hopkinson of the Citizens Party expressed concern about the need for such a large scale reclamation. Some critics said the creation of a commercial park would have been a better idea.

The Hong Kong Tourist Association welcomed the opportunities the development would create to promote tourism. "The new sports stadium would enable Hong Kong to stage more international events", said spokesman Peter Randall.

Shanghai: China's future Manhattan?

▶ **How might the development of Shanghai's Pudong Economic Zone help to transform the city into becoming once more one of the world's major financial centres?**

A Shanghai's skyline

In 1936 Shanghai was the seventh largest city in the world. At that time it benefited from being one of China's five **open cities**, which meant that it traded with western countries.

After the People's Republic of China was established in 1949, Shanghai declined as a city. It only began to flourish again after 1978 when the country adopted a more open policy towards the outside world.

Two major planning schemes have been undertaken to develop Shanghai:

- the creation of **satellite towns** to decentralise the city centre and to encourage new industries;
- the establishment of the Pudong New Area since 1990. This is a previously relatively undeveloped site of 35 square km, immediately opposite the Bund, Shanghai's central business district.

The Pudong is being developed with the following main aims:

- to encourage foreign investment. Overseas firms which establish here have all the benefits of China's Special Economic Zones, as well as opportunities to deal through foreign banks located within the Pudong.
- coordination with Shanghai's congested central area to solve the city's chronic urban problems.

The development of the Pudong is an important step in re-establishing Shanghai as a major world city. The area also has strategic importance for China, because its growth should stimulate the development of the Yangtze River region as a whole.

Percentage share		
	1990	2000
GNP	8.1	25.0
Retailing	4.0	30.0
Population	10.4	14.8

B Pudong's increasing share of Shanghai's wealth and population

C The location of Pudong in Shanghai

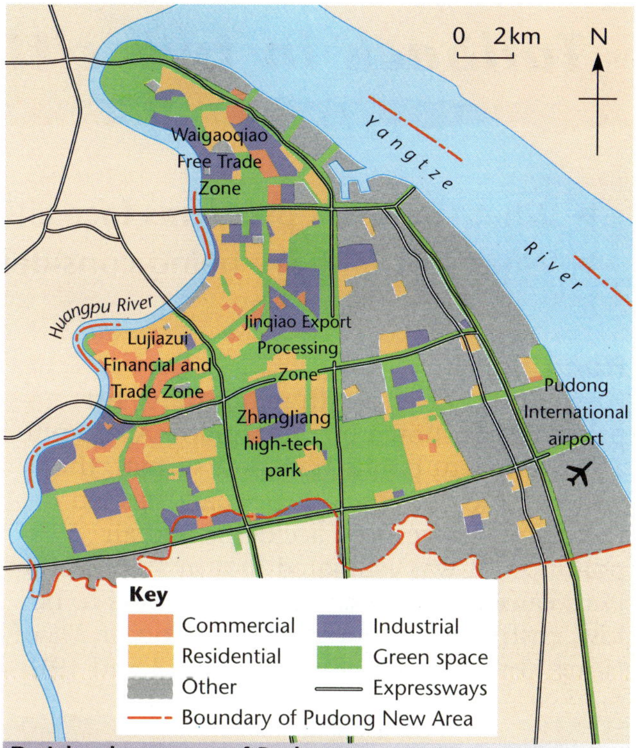

D A land-use map of Pudong

	1990	2000
GNP (RmB million)	6 020	50 000
Primary sector (RmB million)	220	500
Secondary sector (RmB million)	4 590	24 500
Tertiary sector (RmB million)	1 210	25 000
Exports (US $ million)	570	6 100
Population (million)	1.34	1.80

E The planned growth for Pudong, 1990 – 2000

- Jinqiao Export Processing Zone – export processing industries. Areas will be reserved for industries relocated from the city.
- Lujiazui Financial and Trade Zone – finance, commerce and tertiary industries, and extension of the Bund.
- Zhangjiang high-tech park – high-technology industries and universities.
- Waigaoqiao Free Trade Zone – export processing industries, warehouses, port.

F Functions of Pudong's Special Development Zones

FACT FILE

Big business

With a population of more than 13 million, Shanghai is China's largest metropolitan area. It is also one of the world's largest ports. The city's gross domestic product increased by 12.7% between 1996 and 1997.

The Pudong area has many important advantages as an area for development. For example, Shanghai people are very enterprising, the city's labour force is highly trained compared with that in other areas of China; Shanghai is an important centre for scientific research.

Seventy nine of the world's leading 500 multinational corporations had invested in the Pudong area by 1997. In June of that year a joint venture between the Shanghai Auto Corporation and General Motors was established in Pudong, the largest project ever imported by the area.

In the first seven years of its development 204 high-rise buildings, 17 storeys or higher, mushroomed in Pudong.

Tailback in two cities

▶ What transport problems face cities like Beijing and Hong Kong?
▶ What solutions are being considered?

Hong Kong

Hong Kong is a city with major transport problems, as shown by photograph A. Despite a very efficient public transport system, the vast volume of traffic on the roads has led to increasing congestion, accidents and air pollution. It was estimated that in 1996 traffic jams caused 124 million working hours to be lost, costing the economy £1.5billion or 2% of Hong Kong's GDP (see also pages 18 and 19).

B Increasing car ownership

Year	1948	1958	1968	1978	1988	1998
Private cars	5 758	24 378	69 062	142 049	178 234	359 694
Total vehicles	10 051	35 305	109 654	233 150	347402	569 411

C Average daily passenger journeys

1997	Bus	Train	Taxi	Car	Tram	Ferry
Number (1000s)	5 787	3 281	1 298	1 081	291	196
%	48	27	11	9	3	2

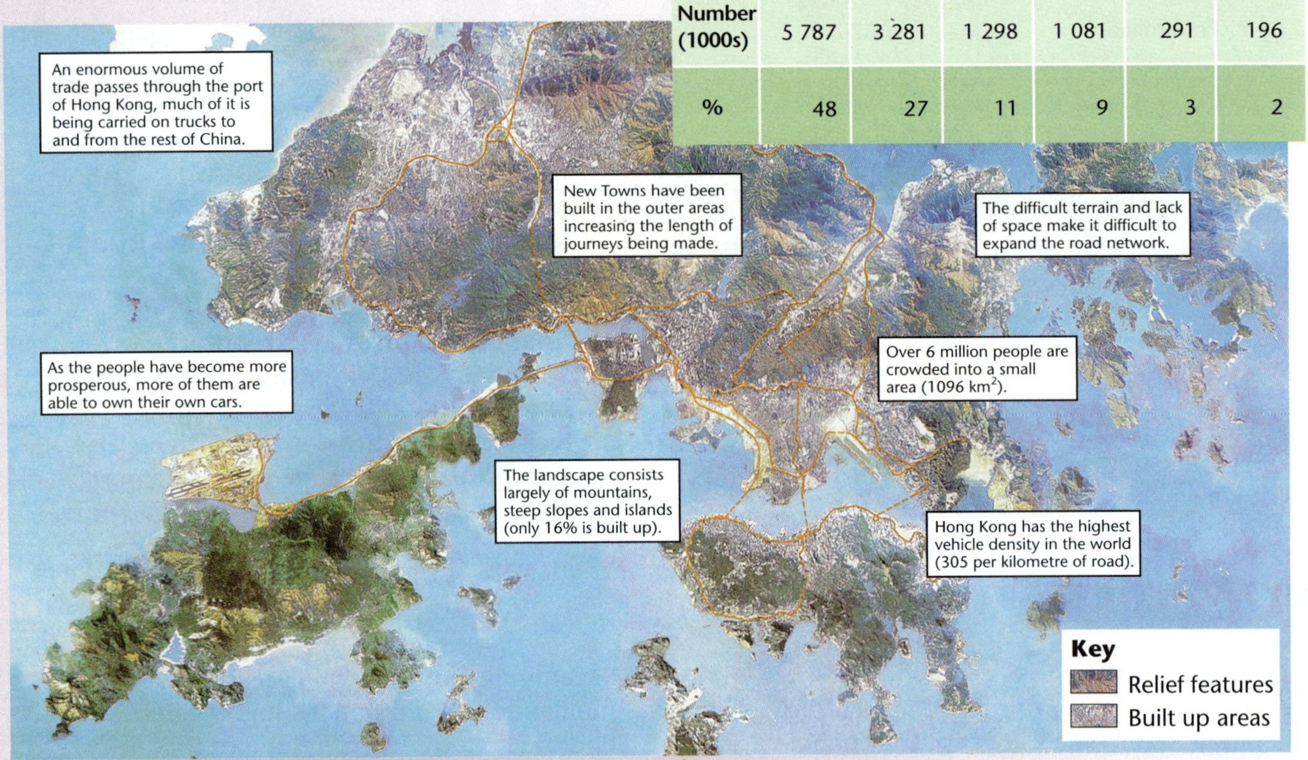

A Satellite photograph of Hong Kong showing major roads

Strategies considered, or already in use, include:

- bus only lanes (localised only, so not really effective);
- staggered working hours and working from home;
- higher charges at some toll tunnels to encourage motorists to use less congested routes;
- 40% extension of the railway system;
- park-and-ride schemes from railway stations in the outer areas;
- higher road tax, fuel tax and registration fees;
- restrictions on the number of new car licences;
- an Electronic Road Pricing scheme (ERP), where motorists pay to use busy stretches of road.

Beijing

Beijing has not always had the traffic problems that you would expect in a city of over 12 million people. In 1985 private cars in the city were virtually unknown. Cycling is said to be about 20% quicker and more comfortable than the overcrowded public buses and trains in the rush hour. However, as more people can afford a car, the usual problems of congestion and pollution are increasing, with the added issue of conflict between cars and bicycles on the major roads.

D Cyclists in Beijing

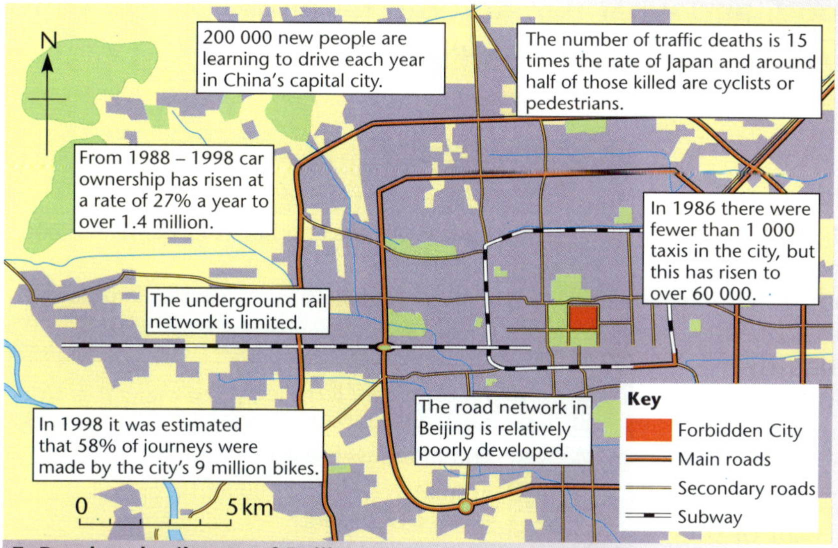

E Road and rail map of Beijing

Strategies considered, or already in use include:

- encourage greater use of public transport, rather than bicycles;
- ban bicycles from busy sections of road from 7 - 8 am;
- remove lines of trees that separate bicycle lanes from car lanes on many routes;
- build four ring roads to speed up traffic flow;
- ban odd or even numbered vehicles on certain days of the week;
- transport more cargo at night;
- get more people to observe traffic regulations.

FACT FILE

Computers to the rescue?

The government of Hong Kong completed a transport study in 1999 to look at future transport strategies for the region over the next 20 years. The main aims were to improve the transport infrastructure, to expand and give priority to public transport and to manage road use more effectively.

The Transport Bureau has proposed a variety of ways to reach these goals and one section of their report is concerned with the use of information technology in traffic management. Computers are already used to co-ordinate traffic signals, and the potential for much greater use of such technology, to make better use of the road network in particular, is recognised. Under consideration are systems to:

- provide commuters with information about best routes to given destinations;
- advise motorists about traffic conditions and delays due to accidents, road works, etc.
- inform drivers about availability of parking spaces;
- integrate toll and parking payment systems.

Information for the above services could be provided by roadside messages, or by in-car map and message systems. These possibilities are in addition to the idea of Electronic Road Pricing, for which feasibility studies have already been conducted. However, the physical geography of Hong Kong limits the choice of alternative routes, making it impossible for motorists to avoid the most popular, congested roads.

(Transport Bureau, Government of the Hong Kong Special Administrative Region.)

3 CHALLENGE OF THE ENVIRONMENT

China's sorrow

▶ What causes a river to flood, and what damage can be done?
▶ What can people do to reduce the risk of flooding?

Flooding on the Yellow River

The Huang He, or Yellow River, is the second longest in China (over 5000 km long). The river has flooded in three out of every four years in the past, causing widespread destruction and thousands of deaths. In both 1889 and 1938, it is thought that flooding killed almost one million people. No wonder the river is also known as 'China's sorrow'.

Why does it flood?

The river floods when it cannot carry all of the water and the **load** in its channel. The flow of water into the river comes from precipitation and melting snow in the drainage basin. The load is mostly made up of fine, yellow soil, called **loess**. Each year the river washes away about 1.6 billion tonnes of soil from the drainage basin. Look at diagrams **B** and **D** for further information.

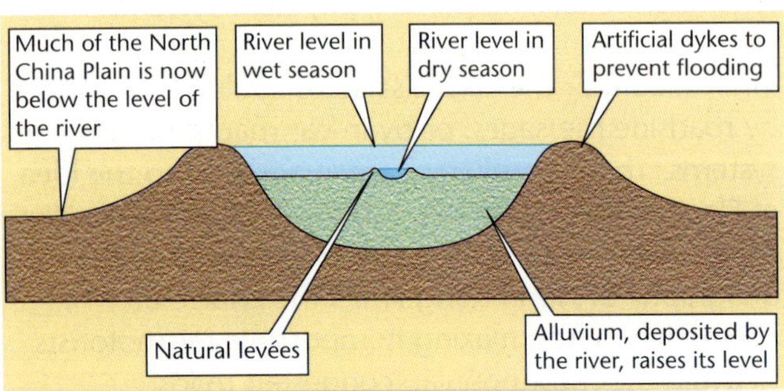

B Cross-section of the river in its lower course

MAY	Snow melts in the mountains. The wet season begins.
JUNE	River level rises and bursts its banks in 8 000 places. Plans are made to evacuate 876 000 people.
JULY	1 million local people work to strengthen the defences. An estimated 8 million people affected; 5 million hectares of farmland are submerged.
AUGUST	End of the wet season. Estimated deaths 2 500 and economic losses £12 billion.

A A typical wet season (1996)

C Dykes on the Yellow River help prevent flooding

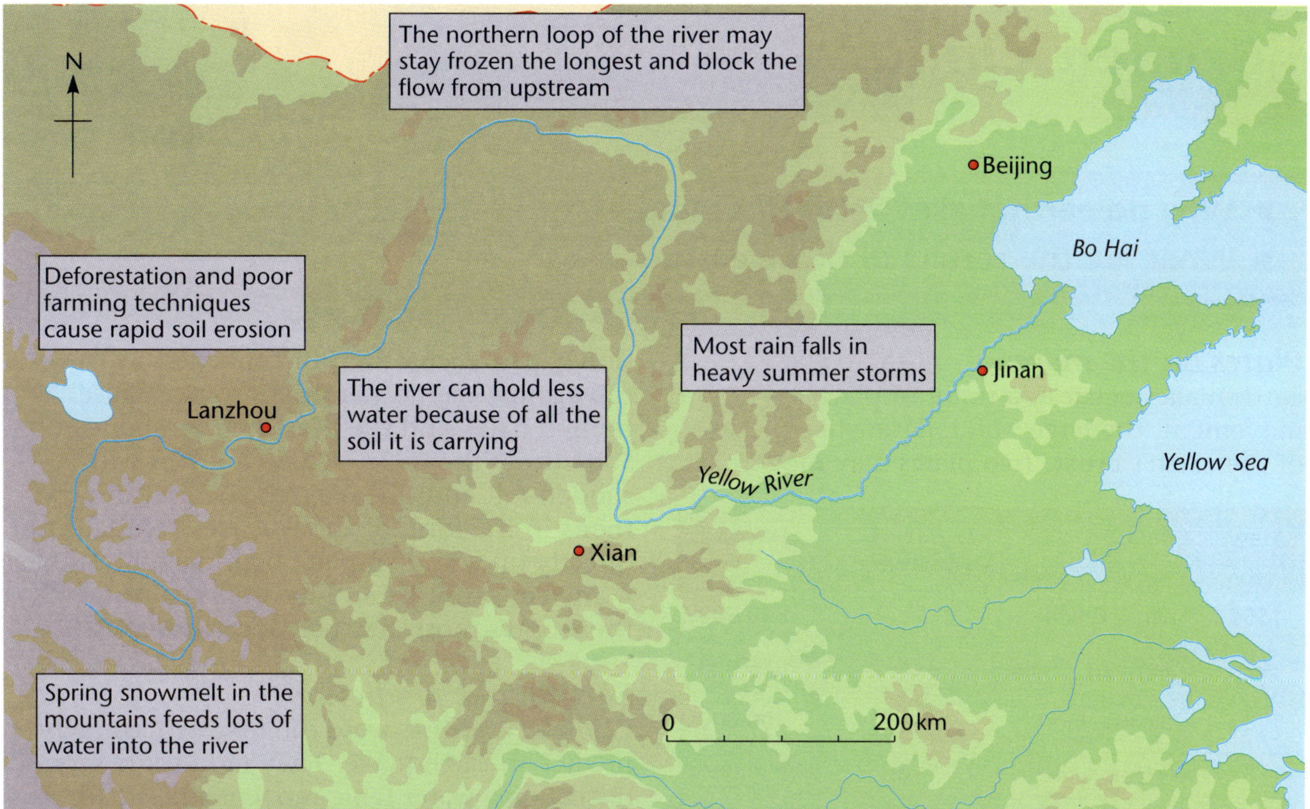

D **Some causes of flooding on the Yellow River**

Flood management

In the past the people relied on **dykes**, built along the sides of the river to prevent flooding. Widespread tree planting is now being encouraged and the farmers are using **terraces** on the steeper slopes. Both of these measures slow down surface flow and reduce **soil erosion**.

Many dams have been built along the river and its **tributaries** to hold back water in the flood season. They also provide water and **hydro-electric power** for people, farms and industry. Navigation is also improved as the river is deeper in the dry season.

The river has been straightened and dredged in many places to speed up the flow of the water to the sea.

FACT FILE

Too much or too little?

Although flooding along the Yellow River may get most of the attention in the press, it also suffers from other problems. Pollution of the river's water and drying up of the lower course are preventing further development in the area. The major cities of Sanmenxia, Poyang and Xinjiang have all recently stopped using the river as a source of drinking water because it is so dirty.

Over the past 20 years the lower course of the river has dried up for an average of 50 days a year, but in 1996 the lower 1 000 km of the river was dry for 150 days.

The channel was dry for an incredible 226 days in 1997 and the 1998 drought lasted for 133 days. Over 30 billion m^3 of Yellow River water is used every year, 92% of it for irrigation, and over 60% of that is lost before it reaches the crops. The World Bank warns that the water shortages pose a greater long-term threat than the floods and conservationists have drafted new laws to protect the river. The price of water has been increased to encourage people to use less and there are even plans to divert water huge distances from other, wetter parts of the country.

Broken China?

- ▶ Why do earthquakes occur in China?
- ▶ What are the results of these earthquakes?

Plates on the move

Earthquakes occur as a result of plate movement, the large, solid, jigsaw-like pieces of the earth's **crust**. Two plates may move slowly past each other for centuries. As they rub against each other, friction may cause them to stick and the pressure then builds up. Sometimes the rocks free themselves with a sudden jolt and this releases energy from the **focus** in the form of shock waves. China is not directly on a known plate boundary, but it has many active **faults** and has suffered some of the world's most destructive earthquakes.

Year	Location	Magnitude (if known)	Deaths
1556	Shansi, China	–	830 000
1976	Tangshan, China	8.0	655 000
1737	Calcutta, India	–	300 000
1138	Aleppo, Syria	–	230 000
1927	Xining, China	8.3	200 000
856	Damghan, Iran	–	200 000
1920	Gansu, China	8.6	200 000
893	Ardabil, Iran	–	150 000
1923	Kwanto, Japan	8.3	143 000
1290	Chihli, China	–	100 000

A Most destructive known earthquakes on record, (USGS National Earthquake Information Centre)

Earthquake prediction

Chinese scientists were the first to accurately predict an earthquake. They monitored ground distortions, water table movements, small tremors and animal behaviour. On 4 February 1975, the **seismologists** informed the government that a quake was due near Haicheng. Later that evening, after over 1 million people had been evacuated, there was a **magnitude** 7.8 earthquake. The China Daily newspaper recently reported that 18 out of 24 earthquakes were correctly forecast in a study that measured the rise in temperature of thc earth's crust, from satellites.

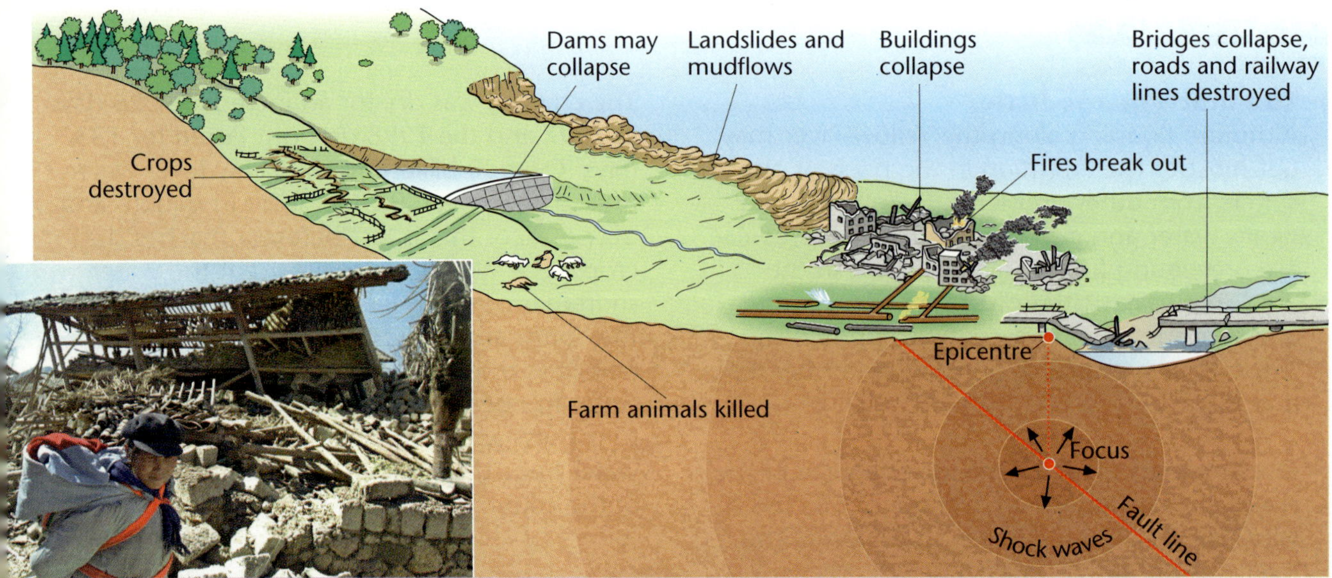

B The primary effects of an earthquake

The destruction of Tangshan

Unfortunately, the massive earthquake which destroyed Tangshan in July 1976 was not predicted. The city lies next to a fault line that runs through northern China and was flattened by a magnitude 8.0 earthquake. It is thought that around 655 000 people were killed (China puts the number at 250 000). Several factors contributed to the high loss of life:

- the **epicentre** was directly beneath a densely populated area;
- the city was built on soft **alluvium** which behaves like quicksand when it is shaken;
- the brick-built buildings of the city were not shake-resistant and collapsed easily;
- the quake struck at night and most victims were buried and crushed as they slept.

The summer heat and heavy rainfall that followed the quake brought problems as diseases spread through the refugee camps. It was days before relief agencies could get water, food, medicine, clothing and shelter to the survivors. These threats to life that follow the actual earthquake are called secondary effects.

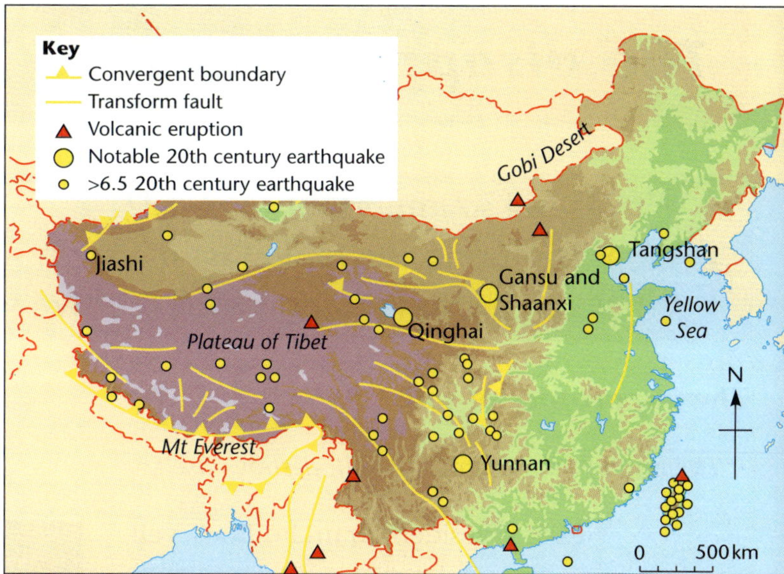

C Seismic activity in China

D Jiashi, 24 January 1997

Two powerful earthquakes struck the Jiashi region 3 000 km west of Beijing yesterday. At least 50 people have been killed as buildings were flattened and army medical teams are treating the hundreds of injured in open-air clinics. The earthquakes measured 6.4 and 6.3 on the **Richter scale** and destroyed 15 000 houses. 2 500 families are sleeping in tents or on school floors. Reports say that 3 360 livestock animals were also killed. Officials fear that the cold winter weather (-15°C), lack of food, diseases, and difficulty getting supplies into the remote area may lead to more deaths.

Associated Press

FACT FILE

Chinese earthquakes measuring over 7 on the Richter Scale

Years	Number of Earthquakes	Number of Deaths
1895 – 1906	10	no exact figure known
1920 – 1934	12	250 000 – 300 000
1946 – 1955	14	10 000 – 20 000
1966 – 1976	14	270 000
1988 - 1998	9	40 000

(From the *Beijing Review*)

The disappearing soil

▶ Why is soil so important to us all?
▶ What is causing the rapid loss of soil in some places?
▶ What can be done to prevent excessive soil erosion?

The importance of soil

"The nation that destroys its soil, destroys itself."

ex-US President Franklin Roosevelt.

Soil is the layer of **weathered** rocks and decomposed vegetation at the ground surface. It is vital to all of us because it is where plants grow, and so it is where we get our food from. It takes between 200 and 1000 years to form 2.5 cm of topsoil and some of the soil is always being removed by the wind and the rain. The actions of people have increased the natural rate of **soil erosion**, so that globally about 75 billion tonnes of **topsoil** are being lost every year. It has been calculated that this loss of soil costs over £250 billion a year, or nearly £50 for every person on earth.

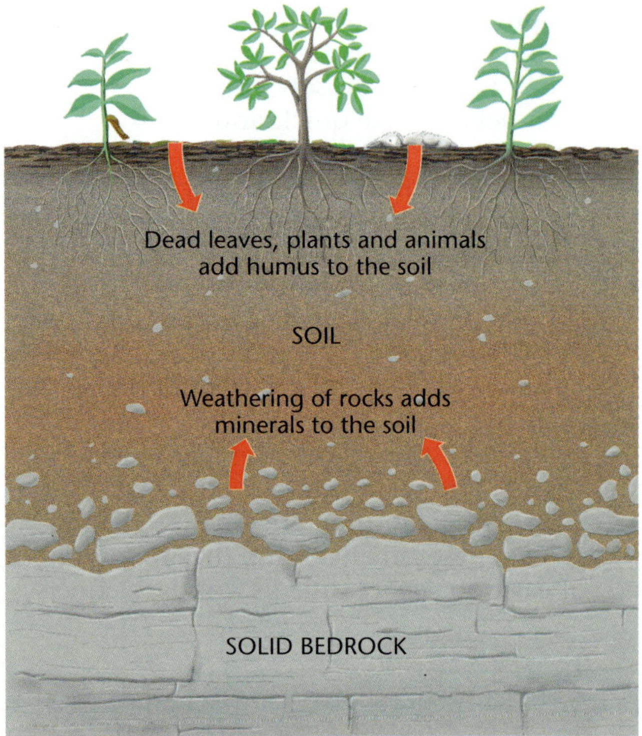

A A typical soil profile

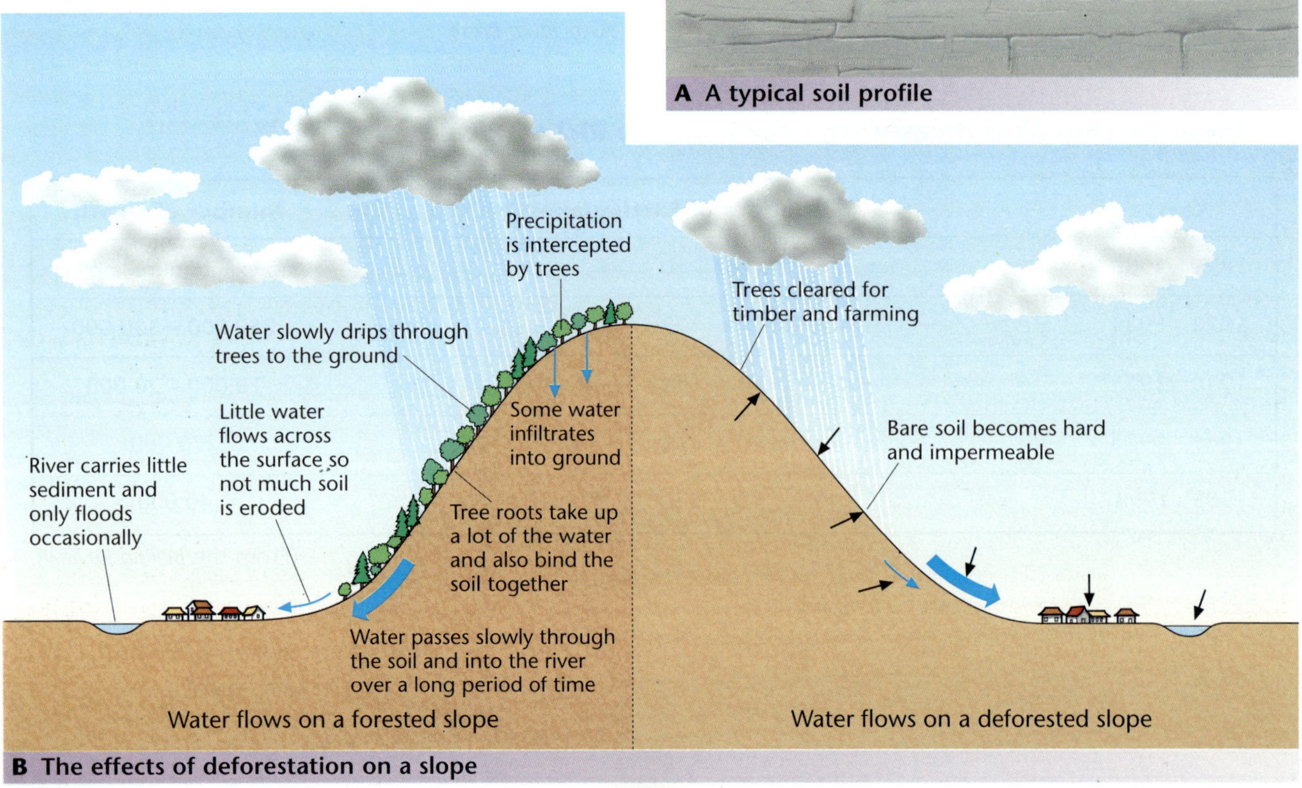

B The effects of deforestation on a slope

The situation in China

China is losing about 30-40 tonnes of **topsoil** per hectare per year, with only about 1 tonne per hectare being formed. It is estimated that the losses of nutrients through soil erosion are nearly the same as the amount of fertilizer that the country produces each year.

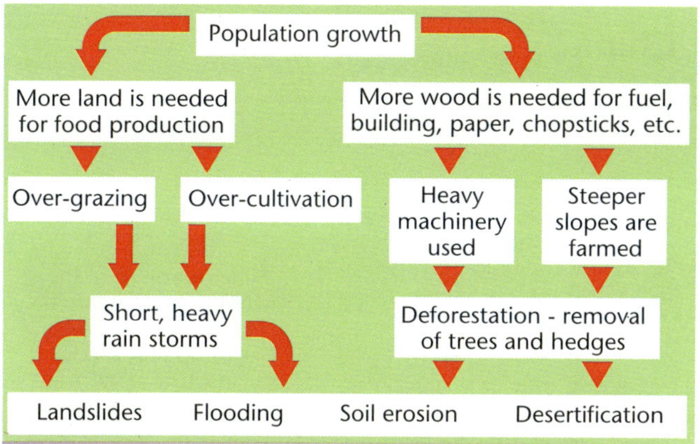

C How the problems arise

D Terracing increases yields and helps reduce soil erosion

Losing the loess

The Loess Plateau is a region along the Yellow River, about the size of France and with a similar population. Loess is the name of the fine, silty, fertile soil of the area. The soil holds little water in the dry climate and is easily eroded by wind and water, particularly if the steeper slopes are farmed. It is claimed that when farmers are working on the Loess Plateau, the increased dust in the air can be detected in Hawaii, 5000 km away.

The World Bank project

The **World Bank** is assisting China in a project to increase agricultural production in the area and to reduce the amount of soil being lost into the Yellow River (about 1 billion tonnes a year). The project will:

- take 100 000 hectares of the most vulnerable land out of cultivation;
- plant 270 000 hectares with grass, shrubs or trees, depending on the conditions;
- terrace 83 000 ha of slopes between 5° and 20°. Terracing can increase yields by three times as well as reduce soil erosion by 95%;
- construct small earth dams that can hold back 90% of the water and nearly all of the soil. They also provide water for villages and for irrigation;
- provide funds for education training and research.

FACT FILE

The importance of trees

After the intense flooding of 1998, the Chinese government announced that lack of forests was China's biggest natural resource problem. The removal of tree cover was said to be responsible for economic and social problems, as well as environmental ones. The authorities banned logging in the upper Yangtze River basin after soil erosion on deforested slopes, resulting in silting of river beds, was blamed for the flooding.

In Sichuan province, the loggers were supposed to plant a new sappling for every tree cut down since 1981, but they rarely did. Now logging is banned and this will cost 45 000 people their jobs. The loggers were immediately re-employed to replant the forests, but drivers and other workers are no longer required. They were to be given new jobs in hotels and state-run businesses and officials talk enthusiastically about developing orchards, tourism and manufacturing industry, but many believe that this will not happen.

The cost of timber in Sichuan has already risen and vast government subsidies will be needed to support the economy for years to come. The region is naturally beautiful but the inaccessible valleys, with narrow roads frequently blocked by landslides, are hardly ideal for attracting new industries.

Is China choking?

- ▶ Why is air quality so poor in parts of China?
- ▶ What is happening as a result of this poor air quality?

Trouble in the air

In China enormous amounts of pollutants are released into the atmosphere. This can affect the health of the people and the quality of the environment. The industrial cities suffer the most, but pollution can also be carried to other parts of the country and beyond. Some gases released may increase the **greenhouse effect** and some damage the ozone layer. Others result in the problem of **acid rain**.

Cancer of the respiratory system is the biggest single killer in urban China.

The air in 90% of China's cities fails to meet the government's clean air standards.

Nine out of 10 of the world's most polluted cities are in China. (World Resources Institute, 1999)

Year	1942	1949	1960	1970	1980	1990	1995
Million tonnes	70	32	265	360	600	1 004	1 298

A Increasing coal use in China

B Many areas of China are heavily polluted

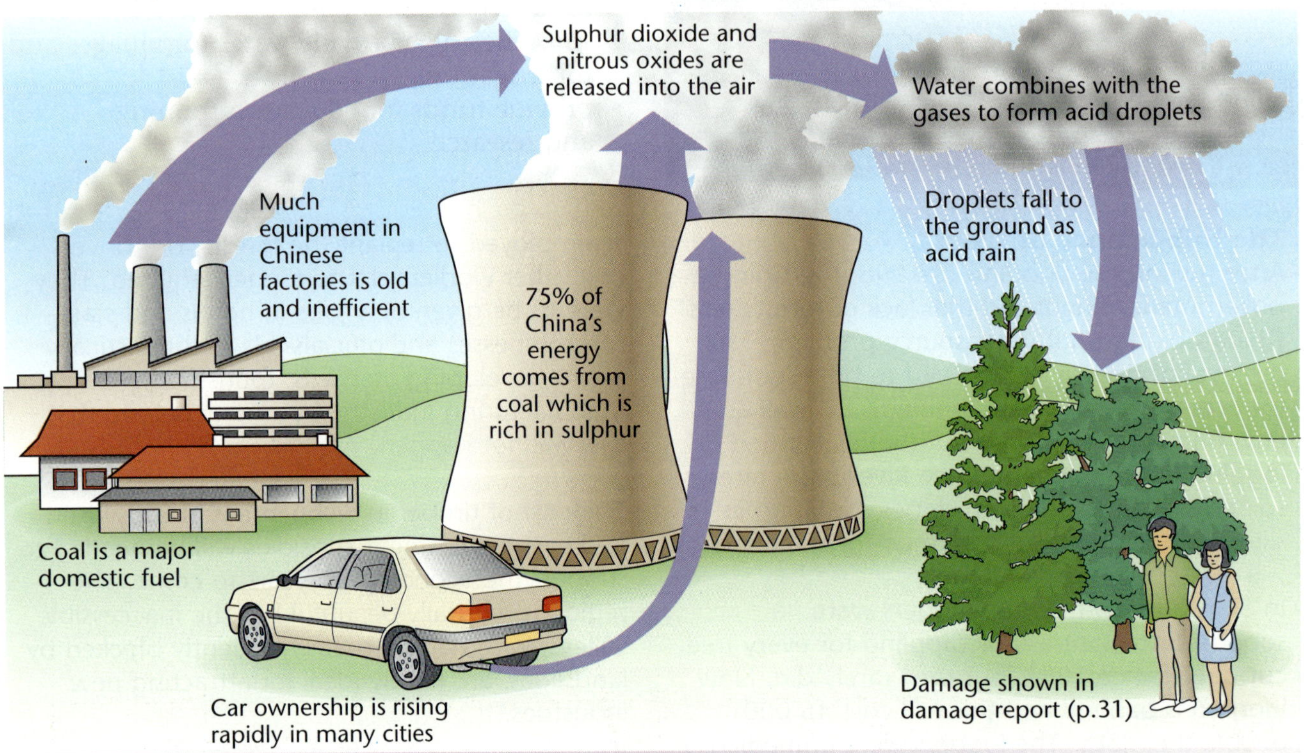

C Production of acid rain

Damage report

PEOPLE

Toxic metals dissolve into the water supply, damaging peoples' nervous system. Lung cancer and **respiratory diseases** increase.

SOIL AND PLANTS

Nutrients such as calcium and potassium are leached out of the soil. Plants, crops and trees can be damaged or killed.

WATER

Increased acidity in lakes and rivers harms fish and plant life. Fish may suffocate or be unable to reproduce.

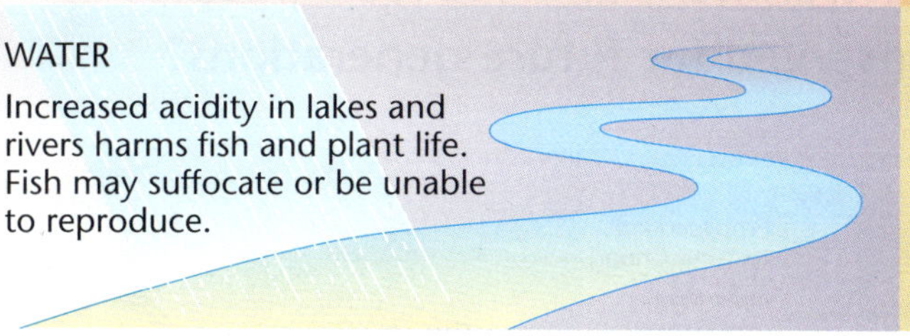

STRUCTURES

Buildings and other structures can be corroded by the acid rain.

The worst sufferer?

PATIENTS NAME: Chongqing, in Sichuan Province

ALSO KNOWN AS: China's dirtiest city

MAIN CAUSE OF SICKNESS: emits 800 000 tonnes of sulphur dioxide into the atmosphere yearly.

SYMPTOMS:

- double the regional rate of asthma and lung cancer;
- thousands of hectares of forest destroyed;
- four species of trees have died and had to be replaced along the city streets;
- paint peels off buildings three times faster than in Beijing;
- metal railings and lamp-posts have to be frequently replaced as they corrode.

DIAGNOSIS: "Chongqing is not fit for humans to live in," according to one resident.

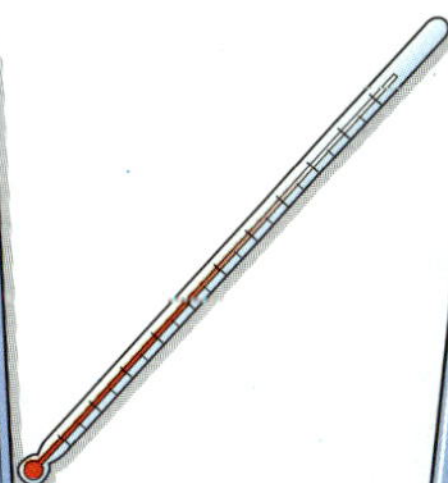

The recommended treatment?

The Chinese government recognises that there is a major problem and is taking the following steps to improve matters:

- £4 billion funding for environmental protection;
- cleaner coal introduced in some cities;
- natural gas replacing coal in Beijing;
- price of coal increased (subsides reduced);
- tax increases for factories that pollute.

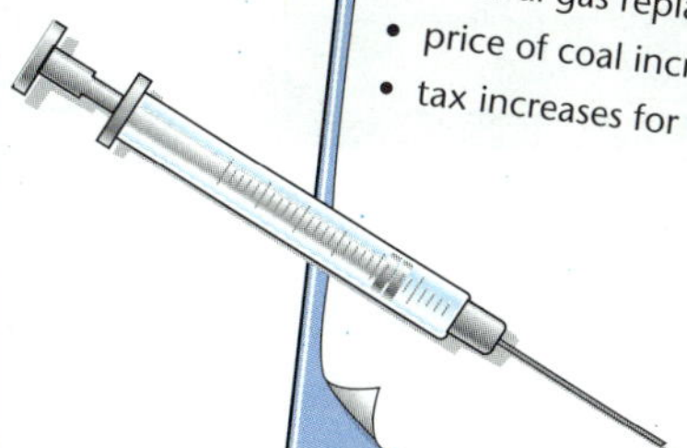

FACT FILE

Measuring air quality

In 1999, 28 Chinese cities began making weekly air quality reports using an Air Pollution Index (API) based on the concentration of major pollutants. The API measures the pollutant concentration and its effect on the environment and human health. It is based on a Chinese and not an international standard. These were the air quality readings for April 16–22, 1999 for selected cities.

Key
NOx Nitrogen Oxides
SO_2 Sulphur Dioxide
TSP Total Suspended Particles

Air quality readings for April 16–22 1999

City	API	Main pollutant	Quality level	City	API	Main pollutant	Quality level
Beijing	184	NOx	III	Lanzhou	342	TSP	V
Chongqing	125	SO_2	III	Shanghai	97	NOx	II
Guangzhou	100	NOx	II	Taiyuan	186	TSP	III
Guilin	52	TSP	II	Urumqi	181	TSP	III

Development versus conservation

- ▶ How have the geographical developments on Hong Kong's Lantau Island affected the economy, the environment and the local people?
- ▶ In what ways might the area be conserved for future generations?

A Chek Lap Kok airport, Lantau Island

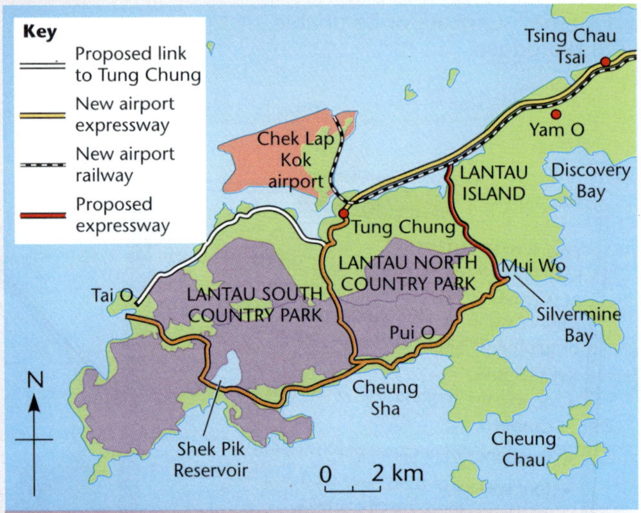

B Map of Lantau Island

Lantau Island is part of the Hong Kong Special Administrative Region. In recent years it has been transformed from a remote rural environment into a very important development area. The island is now linked to the Hong Kong mainland by a suspension bridge and expressway, a railway and a cross-harbour tunnel. One of the world's largest airports, Chek Lap Kok, was opened on Lantau in June 1998. Tung Chung New Town has been built to support the new airport. Hong Kong people have conflicting views about these new developments, summarised in diagram C.

Lantau: facts and figures

- Chek Lap Kok airport has an annual capacity of 35 million passengers (11 million more than Hong Kong's former airport).
- Tung Chung New Town had a population of 20 000 in 1998.
- It is estimated that this population will rise to 200 000 by 2011.
- In the five years before Tung Chung was established (1991-1995), Lantau's population increased by 34 per cent.

Environmental groups in Hong Kong have written a report suggesting ways in which Lantau Island might be conserved in the future. The report's main recommendations are summarised in map **D**.

D Proposals for conservation

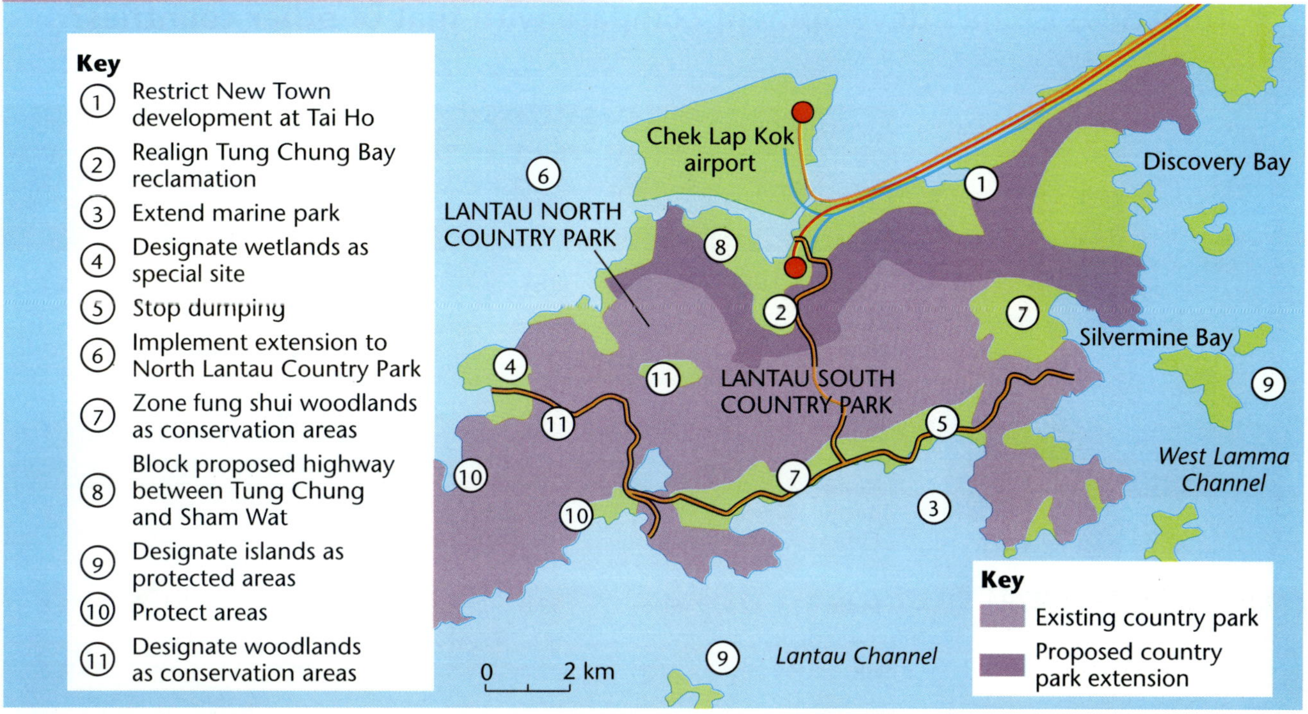

FACT FILE

A new development on Lantau Island?
Plans are being considered for the development of a Disneyland theme park on Lantau, to be located on the coast north-east of Discovery Bay. Some land reclamation would be needed for the site. It is estimated that the new Disneyland could attract two million extra visitors each year to Hong Kong.

Supporters of this development have stressed the economic advantages of the scheme but conservationists are concerned that this will further damage Lantau's natural environment. Shanghai has been proposed as an alternative site. Two factors affecting the final decision will be geographical location and climate.

Some planners have suggested that Disneylands could be located in both Hong Kong and Shanghai. They believe that Hong Kong could cater for visitors from the rest of Asia, and Shanghai for Chinese visitors. However, there is already a Disneyland in Japan which has attracted both Japanese tourists and those from throughout Asia.

4 ECONOMIC DEVELOPMENT

China as a developing country

▶ **How does China's development compare with that of other countries?**

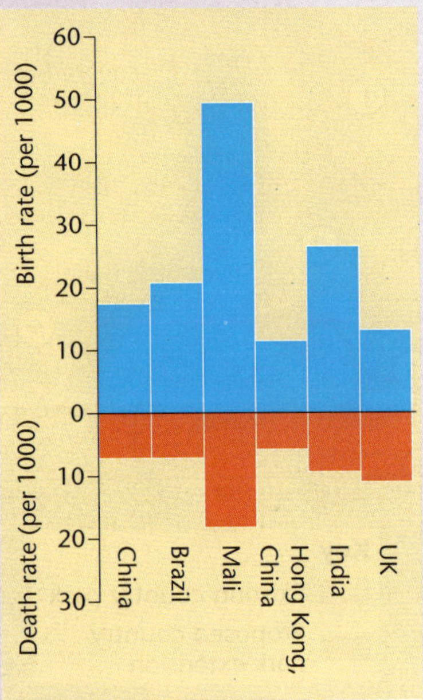

A Birth and death rates, 1995

Country	GNP $ 1995	Life expectancy at birth 1995	Adult literacy rate % 1995	Doctors per 100 000 people 1993	Secondary aged population in school % 1995	Televisions per 1 000 people 1995	Defence expenditure as % of GNP 1996
China	2 935	69.2	81.5	115	67	247	5.7
Brazil	5 928	66.6	83.3	134	45	278	2.1
Mali	565	47.0	31.0	4	9	12	1.8
Hong-Kong, China	22 950	79.0	92.2	144	75	359	3.0
India	1 422	61.6	52.0	48	49	61	2.8
UK	19 302	76.8	99.0	164	100	612	3.0

B Indicators of development

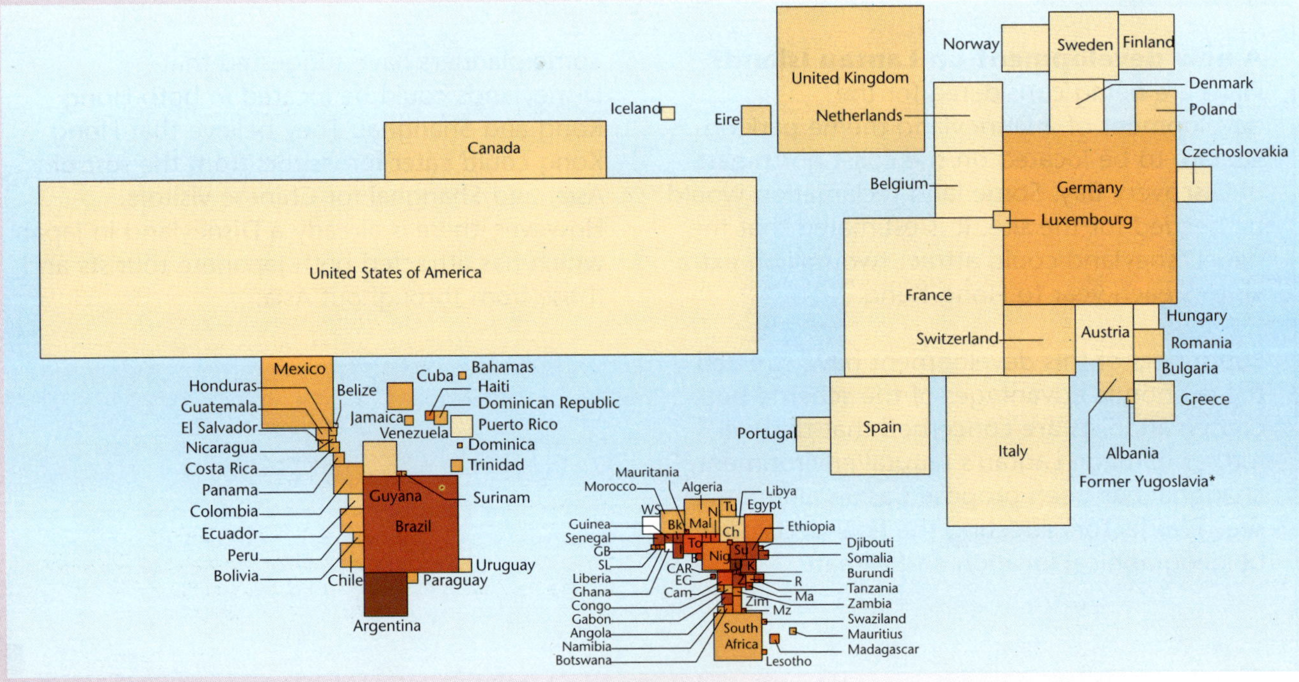

China's rapid economic development

On 1 October 1999, China celebrated the 50th anniversary of the People's Republic. The country has developed remarkably since 1949.

China after 50 years

China, once an agricultural, rural, and peasant nation' is rapidly becoming industrial, urban, and occupationally diversified. The country's growth is one of the most important developments in world affairs over the past 50 years.

China's progress is impressive: increased life expectancy; reduced infant mortality; improved health care; higher literacy rates; higher per capita income; higher per capita grain production; electrification; improvements in transport and communication; expansion of primary; secondary and tertiary education; increase of military might; development of metallurgy; chemical and petroleum industries and so on.

In the past 25 years alone, China's population has increased by more than 400 million people – more than the total population of all of Africa south of the Sahara, or all of Latin America, or all of the former Soviet bloc. This increase has occurred without major domestic strife, without starvation and with a quadrupling of the **gross national product**.

In many places, the past is rapidly fading from view: gleaming modern skyscrapers in the thriving Shenzhen Special Economic Zone are located where peasants in communes ploughed fields with water buffalo as late as 1978. Traffic jams clog Beijing's second ring road where the city wall once stood. Even in mountainous areas, karaoke bars and hawkers selling VCDs and pirated designer jeans line the main streets of small towns and villages. State granaries are now overflowing in regions where massive famines occurred in the 1920s and early 1960s.

South China Morning Post, 1 October, 1999

Rapid economic development creates problems

But this remarkable development has brought its problems, which will need to be solved if China is to become a major world superpower. For example:

- An uneven distribution of wealth, particularly between the country's coastal and interior populations.
- Concerns amongst some people that rapid economic development has led to the adoption of western 'values', for example less concern for the elderly, too much emphasis on money-making and a 'pop' culture.
- An increase in financial corruption in business.
- Inefficient state-owned factories and other businesses.
- Ethnic minorities within China feeling that they are neglected.
- Environmental pollution.

C Percentage share of world GNP and population without access to sanitation, 1990

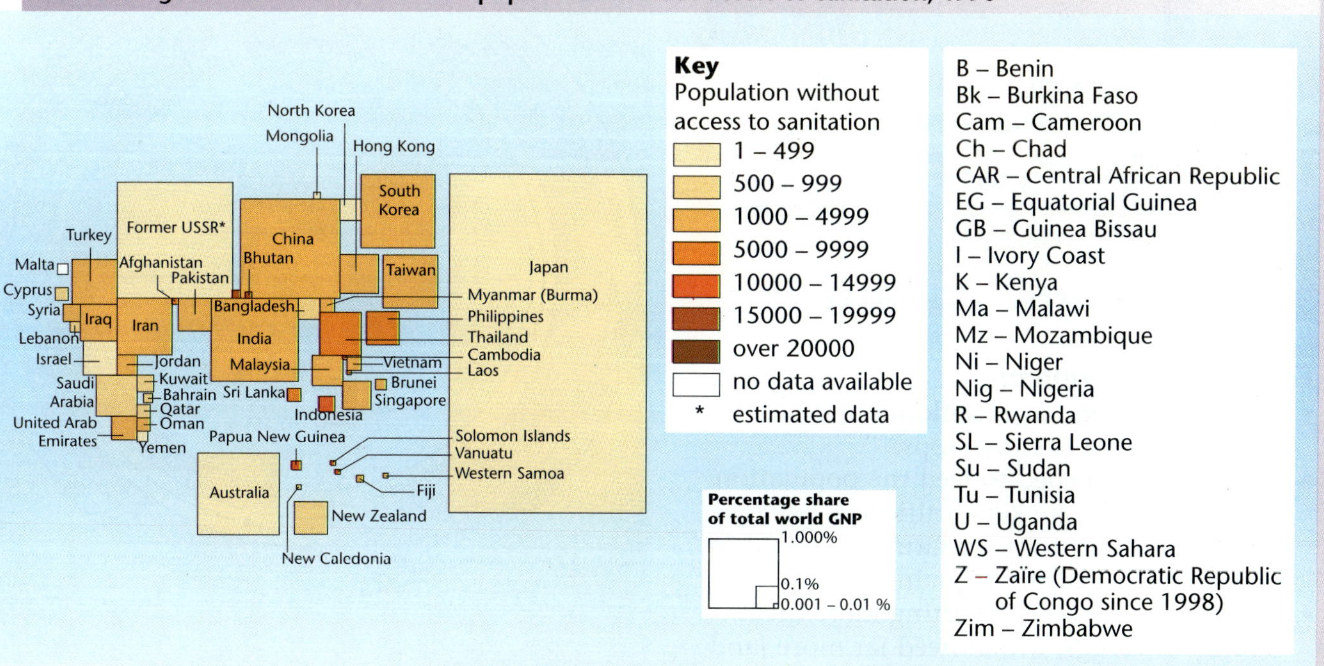

Feeding the population

- ▶ What challenges does China face in order to feed its vast population?
- ▶ How is farming in China organised?

Will there be enough to eat?

China's population has multiplied by five in the last 200 years, but only 25% more land produces food. In fact, China has lost 20% of its arable land since the 1950s and the rate of loss is increasing. Today, it has over 20% of the world's population but less than 10% of its arable land. Many people fear that a famine, like the one of 1959 – 61, in which over 30 million people starved to death, may occur again in the future.

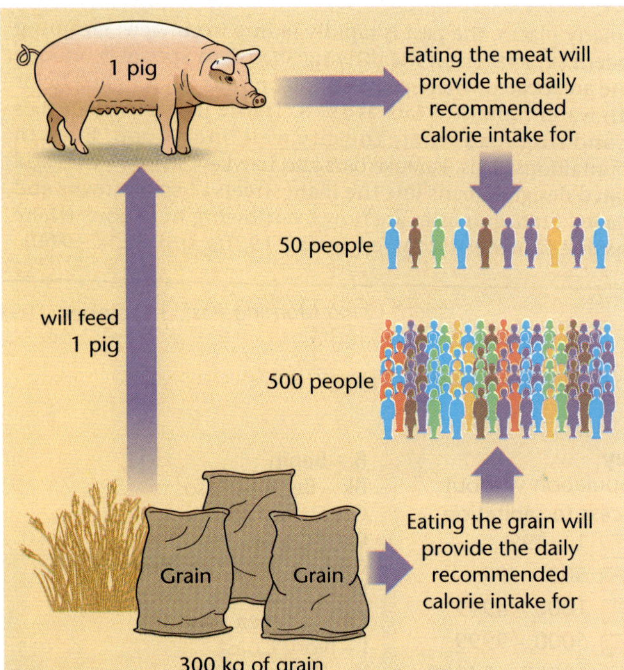

A The implications of China's changing diet

Food supply problems

- Natural disasters, such as floods and typhoons often destroy crops.
- More food is needed to feed the population but grain prices are kept artificially low by government subsidies; so farmers have little **incentive** to grow more grain.
- The Chinese people are eating more meat, poultry and eggs, which need far more land to produce.
- Arable land is being lost to other land uses at a rate of about 500 000 hectares a year.
- Rivers are drying up and the **water table** is dropping in the north of the country as the demand for water increases.

Possible solutions

- A new law states that each province must not reduce the amount of **arable** land it has.
- Create new arable land by terracing hillsides, reclaiming land or converting parks and other open spaces.
- Import large amounts of grain.
- Improve the farming methods and seeds used to increase yields.
- Divert water from the wetter south to the north for irrigation.
- Impose heavy taxes for converting cropland to non-farming uses.

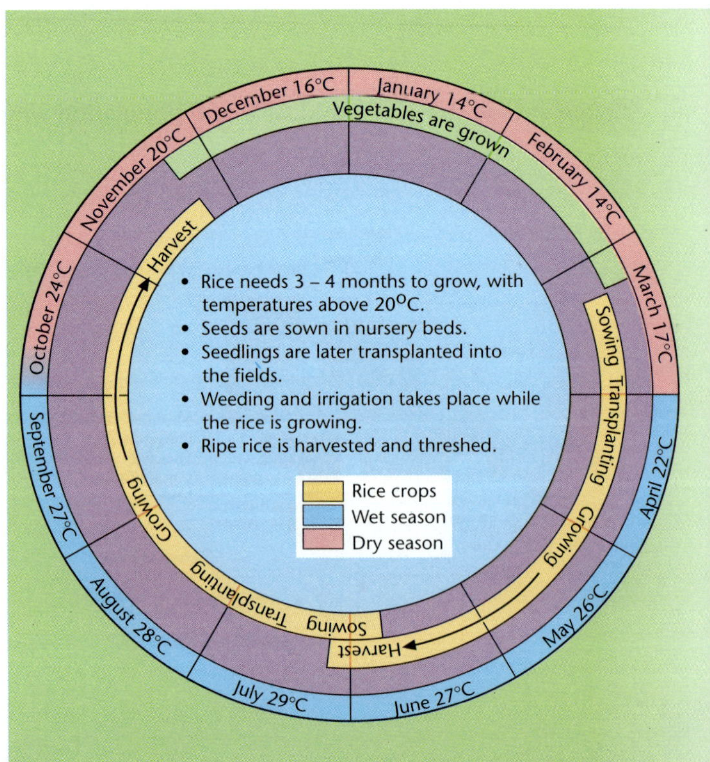

B The farming year on a south China rice farm

C Arable land is being lost at a worrying rate

The old and the new

China has reformed most sections of its economy, and farming is no exception.

The strict communist system has given way to more of a **market economy**, as shown in the boxes below (see also pages 22 and 23).

COMMUNES – THE OLD SYSTEM

- 1 commune = about 2000 households
- Each village (about 200 households) is set a **quota** of how much they have to produce.
- Each family has a small plot of land for their own use.
- Prices are kept low by government subsidies.
- Profits are shared by everyone in the village.
- This system improved production but the ideal crops were often not grown and there was little incentive to produce more.

HOUSEHOLD RESPONSIBILITY – THE NEW SYSTEM

- Individual households are given contracts to lease farmland.
- **Quotas** are set for each piece of land.
- Surpluses are sold by the family.
- Successful groups take up more contracts and can form their own businesses.
- Productivity and profits have increased, but so have prices as subsidies are reduced.
- There has been increased use of fertilisers and a big rise in rural unemployment.

FACT FILE

Rice: the staple food

The diet of most Chinese people, particularly in the south of the country, is based around rice and vegetables. Although China produces by far the greatest amount of rice of any country in the world, it has relatively little to spare for export once the huge population of the country has been fed. Many people will be watching China's future rice production figures very closely indeed.

World rice production, 1998

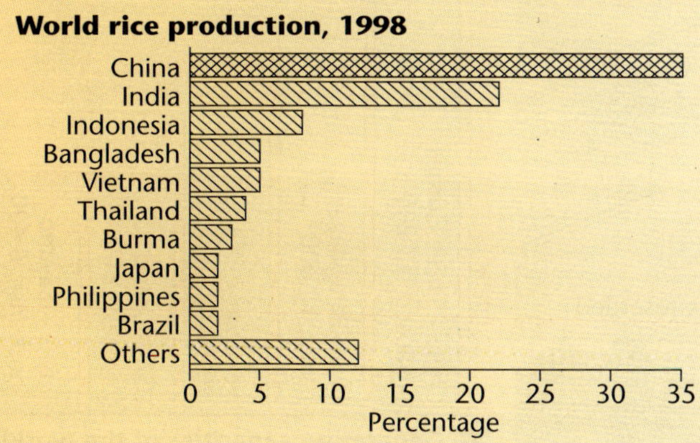

World rice exports, 1998

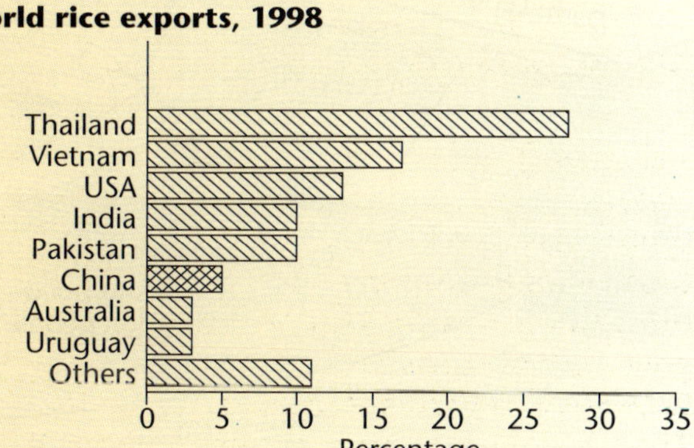

The Three Gorges Scheme

- ▶ Why is energy production from this scheme so important to China?
- ▶ Why is there so much controversy about the scheme?

Rising energy demand

The demand for energy in China is growing rapidly. The population is growing and becoming more affluent. Industries use 65% of China's electricity but frequently operate below capacity due to a shortage of power. Diagram A shows how energy use in China has grown. The figures are forecast to double by 2005, and again by 2020.

Year	1950	1960	1970	1980	1990	1994
Electricity consumption	5	30	76	301	535	780

A Increasing energy use in China (kilowatt hours per person)

Sources of energy

The burning of coal in China causes huge amounts of pollution and results in health problems and damage to the environment (page 30). Coal is also a non-renewable fuel, which will run out at some time, so China is looking at other sources of energy for the future. Is hydro-electric power (HEP) a suitable alternative?

Source of energy	Coal	Oil	Natural gas	Hydro-power
% of total used	75	17.5	1.5	6

B Energy consumption in China, 1996

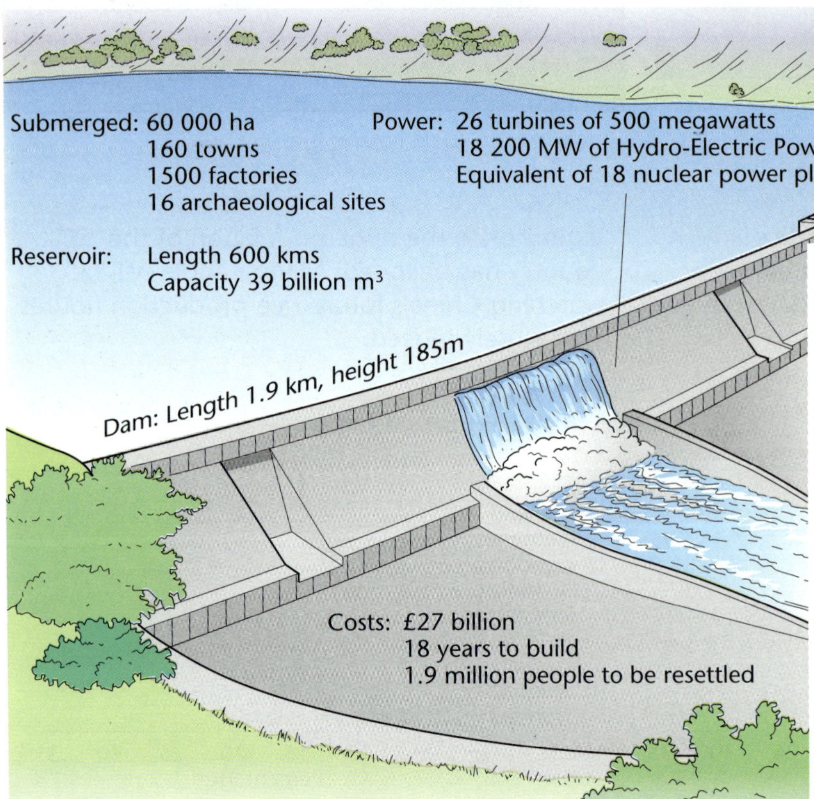

C The Three Gorges Dam: costs and benefits

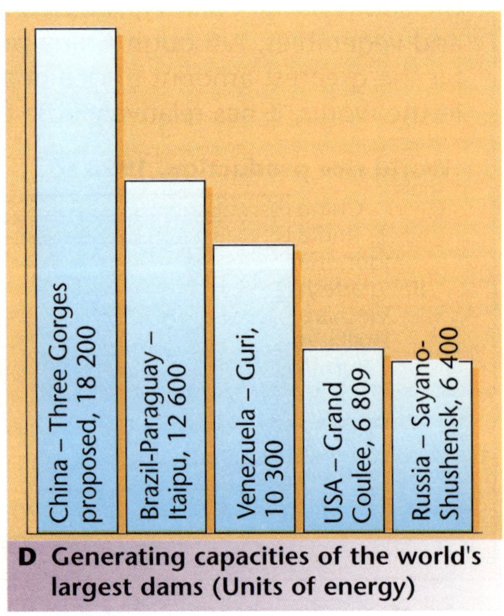

D Generating capacities of the world's largest dams (Units of energy)

A variety of opinions

The Three Gorges Scheme at Sandouping on the Yangtze River is the most ambitious engineering project in China since the building of the Great Wall. There has, however, been strong debate about this Scheme both inside and outside China.

E Yangtze River Gorge

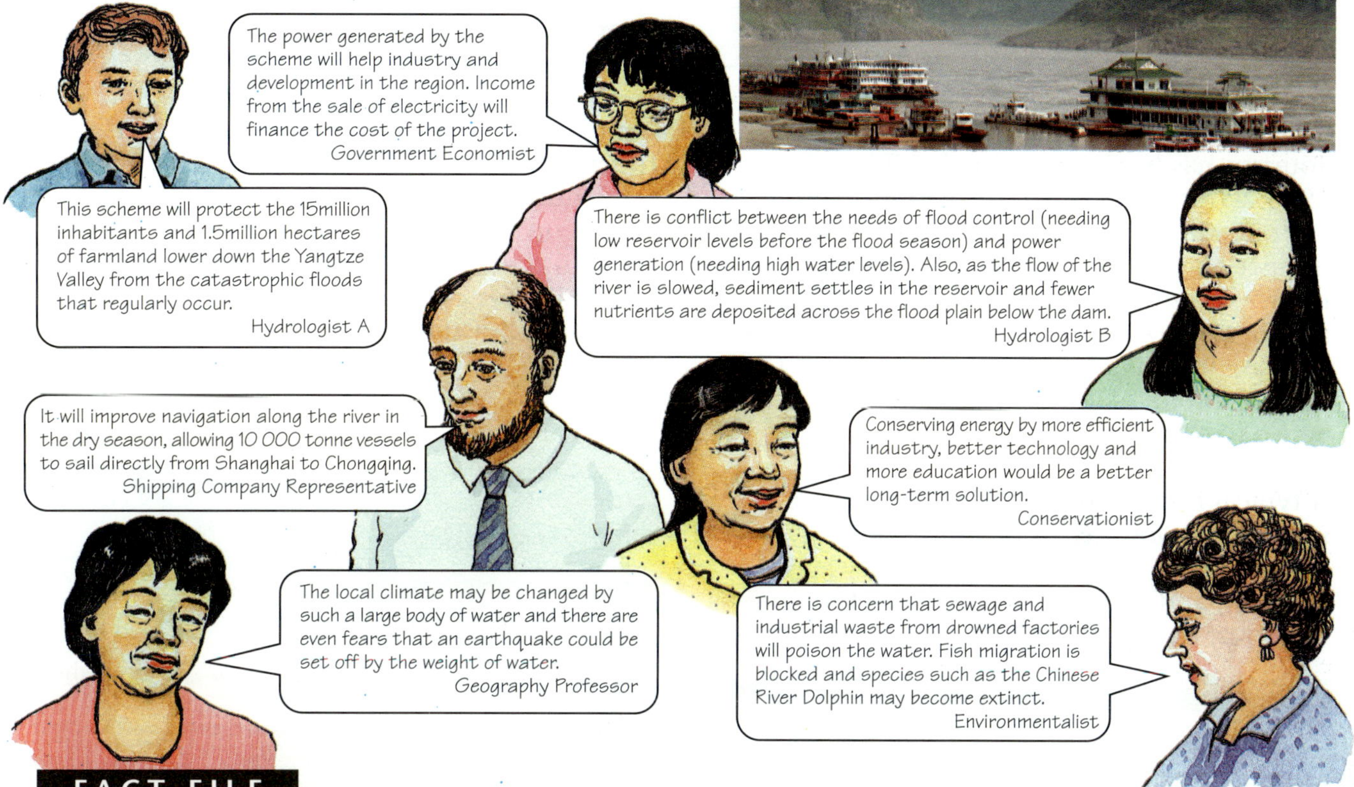

FACT FILE

Dam opposition

Around 19 000 of the world's 40 000 large dams (higher than 15m or a four-story building) are in China. The USA is the second most dammed country, followed by Russia, Japan and India. The number of large dams being built is declining but the countries with the most large dams under construction are currently China, Turkey, South Korea and Japan.

Large dam schemes may be opposed for social, environmental, economic and safety reasons. The main reason for opposition is the huge number of people who lose their land and homes. Between 30 and 60 million people have been displaced by dams, the majority of them in China and India.

More than 13 500 people have been swept to their deaths as a result of dam failures outside China during the 20th century. Two large dams, which burst when a massive typhoon hit the Chinese province of Henan in August 1975, left an estimated 80 000 to 230 000 dead. This disaster was only revealed to the outside world in 1995.

Source: *International Rivers Network*

China's boom industry: tourism

▶ **What have been the benefits and problems of China's rapidly growing tourist industry?**

Advantages of tourism

Tourism has been increasing in China since 1978, when the country opened its frontiers to the outside world. Since then the tourist industry has grown rapidly as a result of improvements in transport and the increased number of hotels. The benefits have been an increase in foreign currency flowing into China and in employment, for example, in the hotel and travel industries.

A typical holiday package for many visitors involves a two-week, four-centre holiday. Visitors fly between cities where they stay (map **B**), and from where they travel to famous historical or scenic sites.

	1980	1985	1990	1996
Total number of international tourists (10 000 persons)	570.3	1783.3	2746.2	5112.8
Foreigners	52.9	137.1	174.7	674.4
Overseas Chinese	3.4	8.5	9.1	15.5
Visitors from Hong Kong, Macao and Taiwan	513.9	1637.8	2562.3	4422.9
Total Foreign Exchange earnings from international tourism (USD 100 million)	6.2	12.5	22.2	102.0

A Growth of tourism in China

(10 000 persons)			
Country	**1990**	**1994**	**1996**
Total	174.7	518.2	674.4
Japan	46.3	114.1	154.9
Korea	5.5	34.0	69.4
USA	23.2	47.0	57.6
Russia	11.0	74.3	55.6
UK	7.9	16.7	20.5
Thailand	6.8	16.4	19.3
Australia	5.0	11.0	13.3
France	5.1	11.2	12.3
Switzerland	1.2	2.8	3.3
New Zealand	1.0	2.0	3.0

The data of Russia in 1990 and 1994 refer to the former USSR.

C Where the visitors to China come from

Some disadvantages

The increase in tourism has created problems at some of these sites.

Overcrowding

Visits are concentrated because the climate in many areas of China creates a high season in summer (see pages 8 and 9).

Tourist wear and tear

Large numbers of visitors create a physical impact on the features they come to see. The steps on the Great Wall, for example, are well worn. Visitors are reminded not to carve on the bricks, but there is often vandalism.

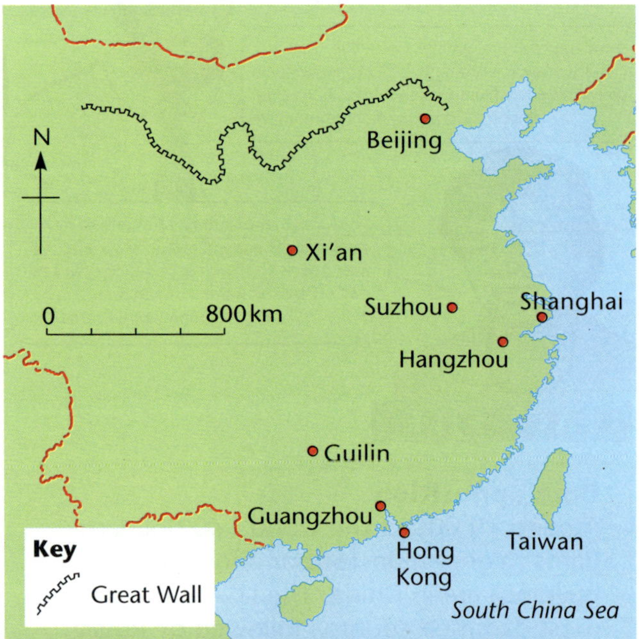

B Main cities where foreign visitors stay

D Tourists on the Great Wall of China

Restoration and development

Restoration of the sites is often needed, for example, an appeal fund has been launched to restore parts of the Great Wall. More visitor centres are needed to explain the history of the sites.

Traffic congestion

Increased tourism has created atmospheric pollution and heavy traffic congestion.

E Tourists on the River Li, Guilin

Tourist honeypot

Guilin is one of China's main tourist honeypots. It is located in Guanxi province. Visitors are attracted to the Li River which is surrounded by a unique form of **Karst** scenery. Tourism has transformed the city. Between 1996 and 1998 a new airport and railway station were opened to cope with the increased number of visitors. Several major new roads were also built.

Number of domestic tourists:	8.4 million
Number of foreign tourists:	450 213
Income from domestic tourists:	14.4 million yuan
Income from foreign tourists	
Sale of products:	2.6 million yuan.
Sale of services:	9.2 million yuan
Increase in number of tourists compared with 1990	
Domestic tourists	11 per cent
Foreign tourists	20 per cent
(Because of the Asia economic crisis, the number of foreign tourists visiting Guilin from January to July 1998 reduced by one third.)	

F Tourism in Guilin: facts and figures for 1997

Month	Jan	Feb	Mar	Apr	May	Jun	Jul	Aug	Sep	Oct	Nov	Dec
Percentage of hotel rooms occupied	29	42	60	61	70	62	63	71	60	78	60	36

G Occupancy rate in Guilin's hotels, 1997

FACT FILE

Top tourist destinations, 1998

Tourist destinations in China, 1997

Rank	City	Income from tourism (10 000 US dollars)
1	Beijing	224 760
2	Shanghai	131 698
3	Guangzhou	102 156
4	Shenzhen	93 006
5	Zhuhai	32 906
6	Xiamen	24 149
7	Xian	20 092
8	Hangzhou	20 078
9	Tianjin	18 009
10	Dalian	17 002
11	Kunming	15 666
12	Guilin	14 014

Changing jobs

- ▶ What is employment structure?
- ▶ How and why is the employment structure in China changing?

Different types of jobs

There are many different kinds of jobs and people often put them into small groups of similar types to make it easier to look for patterns of employment. Putting jobs into groups, or classifying them, can be done in a number of different ways. One classification divides them into primary, secondary or tertiary employment.

- The *primary sector* includes all jobs involved with obtaining **raw materials**, such as food, minerals and timber. Examples of such jobs include fishing and forestry.
- The *secondary sector* contains all those jobs that turn raw materials into something more useful, such as food processing, steel making, engineering or carpentry.
- The *tertiary sector* is made up of jobs that do not produce anything, but they provide a service, such as shopkeepers, police, drivers or nurses.

(Some people add a separate *quaternary sector* which consists of economic activities concerned with getting or giving information, such as research, finance, law, education and the media.)

Country	Primary % (Farming)	Secondary % (Industry)	Tertiary % (Services)	GNP per person (US$)
China, 1952	84	7	9	50 (est)
China, 1996	73	14	13	620
India, 1996	62	11	27	340
Italy, 1996	9	32	59	19 020
Japan, 1996	6	34	60	39 640

Source: United Nations

A Variations in jobs and wealth

Employment structure

The percentage of jobs in each sector is called the employment structure. It will vary between different countries and will change over time (table **A**). In the economically developing countries of the world, the number of jobs in agriculture and manufacturing declined as services increased. In China, even though there have also been changes in the figures, there are still estimated to be more than half a billion people working in agriculture.

Diagram **B** is a triangular graph and this can be used as a way of showing the employment structure of places.

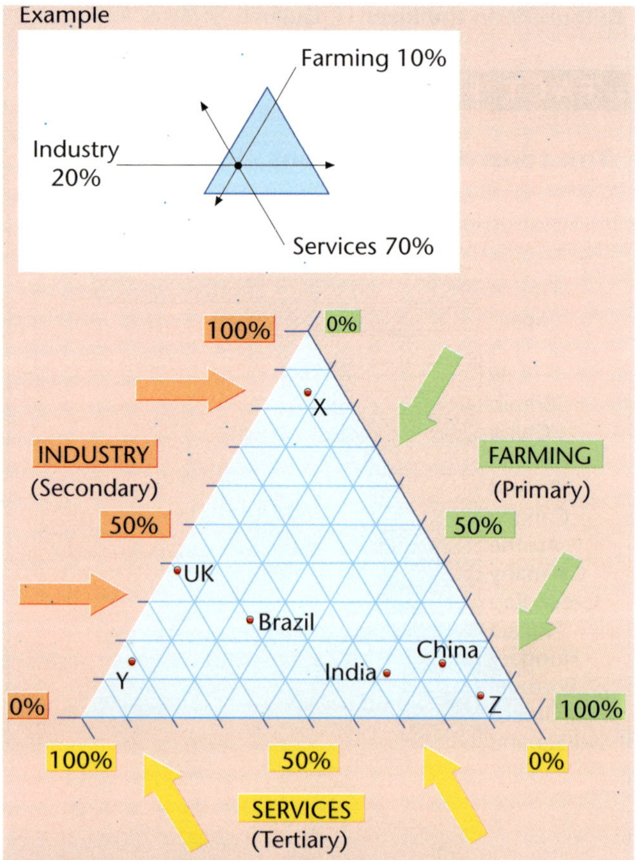

B Triangular graph showing employment structures, 1996

Changes to the employment structure of countries

You may notice a pattern in table **A**. The richer countries (see GNP per person in the last column) have very few people working in the primary sector and have most people working in the tertiary sector. As farming becomes more efficient, the number of labourers employed is reduced. Machines are introduced to replace workers. More money is available for investment into manufacturing industry and people have more time and money to spend on services, such as education, recreation and entertainment.

Increased use of agricultural machinery in China (kilowatts per hectare of cultivated land)		
1985	1990	1995
2.1	3.0	3.8

C More machines, fewer jobs

Tertiary growth

As more people pour into the cities, the Chinese government expects the tertiary sector to expand to 38% of total employment by 2010. Amongst the potential new growth sectors are tourism, real estate, chain stores, information services, advertising, entertainment, banking and insurance.

Primary workers – most Chinese people in the past and in the rural areas today

Secondary worker – most Chinese workers in the towns and cities today

Tertiary worker – most Chinese workers in the whole country in the future?

D The changing nature of employment in China

FACT FILE

Problems at work?

One of the main concerns in China, following the reduction in the state's willingness to fund loss-making enterprises, is the rise in unemployment and its likely consequences. Over 100 million people are still employed by state-owned businesses, but more than half of these businesses are losing huge amounts of money.

In 1998, 12 million new young people entered the labour force, adding to the existing 12.9 million unemployed workers. Over the next 20 years, China will have to create job opportunities for the existing unemployed and for a further 120 million young, often better educated people. The following data illustrate some of the trends which will challenge the Chinese economy in the near future:

China's rising urban unemployment rate		
Year	urban jobless (millions)	unemployment rate (%)
1992	3.939	2.3
1997	5.576	3.1

China's increasing number of laid-off workers	
Year	Number of laid-off workers
1993	3 million
1997	12 million

Increasing levels of education		
	1990, %	1997, %
Proportion of illiterate and semi-literate people aged 15-45	10.4	5.5
People with a college degree and above	1.42	2.53

China's changing rural economy

▶ What has been the impact of the rapid growth of village and township enterprises in China's rural areas?

China has a rural population of 900 million, more than three and a half times the population of the United States. Approximately one third of the people living in rural China are **underemployed**, which explains why 100 million migrate into China's cities for work.

Since the late 1970s there has been a move towards a market economy in the rural areas to try to increase employment. Many small enterprises have been set up, either owned collectively by people in villages or small towns, or run privately.

Some enterprises are small, for example, kerbside selling or workshops manufacturing farm tools and equipment. Others are larger non-agricultural enterprises that obtained loans for factories to process local raw materials or manufacture products. These rural enterprises have brought benefits but also created problems within China's rural areas.

A

Change comes to the village of Nangaoying

Looking out of the window of his new home, He Shengguo sees pleasant open spaces. His family is among the first in Nangaoying, a village near the city of Shijiazhuang in Hebei Province, to move into the new apartment building. More than a dozen 6-storey buildings stand in the new residential area, with gardens, a playground and satellite antennas. It is a sharp contrast to the old village, a scattering of tattered low houses.

Although their status as farmers remain unchanged and each is still given land, they no longer earn most of their living by toiling in the fields all year long. In fact, most of the villagers are now factory workers. These people lived in poverty until ten years ago. Grain used to be the only source of income. The number of young people migrating from the village to large cities such as Beijing has now reduced dramatically.

He Shengguo is the secretary of the village Party Committee. It was he who led the villagers to a better life by launching village enterprises, starting with a small commercial foundry. Huashu Pharmaceutical Factory, the largest local business and the pride of the village, is the largest Terramycin producer in the country and exports 70% of its production overseas.

Most enterprises in Nangaoying are owned and run by the villagers and every village has its own production and distribution system, forming a "village economy" model. The village enterprises have given the people a much better life. For example, Nangaoying now has its own school, hospital, home for the elderly and other public service facilities. Villagers' income is composed of their salary from the village enterprises, distribution of profits from the village and the sale of grain.

It's hard to change the lifestyle and thinking of Nangaoying's farmers, whether they earn their living from the land or by other means. Although agriculture contributes only a small proportion of income, no household seems willing to give up its land. Also, most villagers were slow to accept the apartment buildings. Although subsidies are offered to enhance agricultural production, grain yields remain at medium levels. This makes He Shengguo feel uneasy. He claims that industrial development has been emphasised to the loss of agriculture in recent years.

Eventually, the city of Shijiazhuang will swallow up Nangaoying. A newly built ring road already encloses quite a large part of the village's farmland.

China Today, February 1999

Some problems created by the village and township enterprises

- Loss of cultivated land for food supply.
- Loss of land plus increasing mechanisation means that fewer people are needed in farming.
- In the more remote areas there are high transport costs and difficulties in making market contacts.
- Absence of planning in many areas.
- Lack of effective financial management and corruption in some areas.
- Poor working conditions and high accident rates in some places.
- Destruction of the environment, for example, brick-making destroys the land and lime-making reduces the forest cover.

B The location of Nangaoying

Year	Population (millions)
1984	76
1990	94
1998	135

C Employment in China's village and township enterprises

Sector	% contribution
Electronic communications equipment	17
Machinery	26
Raw coal and cement	40
Food and Beverages	43
Clothing	80

D Contribution of income to China's economy from village and township enterprises

E Making shoes in a township enterprise

FACT FILE

Township enterprises

China's 23.36 million township enterprises have become important to the country's prosperity. In 1997 their annual exports accounted for one-third of the national total.

In 1997 township enterprises in China employed 135 million workers. Within the townships one-third of farmers' income came from this type of employment. In some areas of southern China this proportion was greater than 50%.

Ownership of township enterprises, 1997

Type	Percentage Ownership
State-owned	7.4
Collective	37.1
Private	46.6
Jointly-run	7.0
Foreign funded	0.6
Hong Kong - Macau - Taiwan funded	1.3

Made in China

▶ **Why does a major American company locate a factory in China?**
▶ **What are the benefits for all those concerned?**

The background

Black and Decker is a long established, trans-national American company that manufactures a variety of power tools. In the early 1990s the company lost 25% of its sales in Europe to cheaper, poorer quality, imports from China. Black and Decker decided to form a **joint venture company** with a Chinese firm (Chiaphua), in order to start **manufacturing** in China themselves. This enabled Black and Decker to set up in China quickly, using Chiaphua's existing staff, contacts and expertise, without the difficulties of starting fresh. Black and Decker Chiaphua International Limited (BDCI) began operation in 1996 at a factory in Shajing. Production and sales from the factory in China doubled in the first two years and are continuing to grow impressively.

B Location of Shajing

The manufacturing system

The **manufacturing** system consists of inputs, processes and outputs. For BDCI the inputs come from a variety of locations worldwide. However, 60% or more of the materials used are from China, since this avoids having to pay European Union import duties.

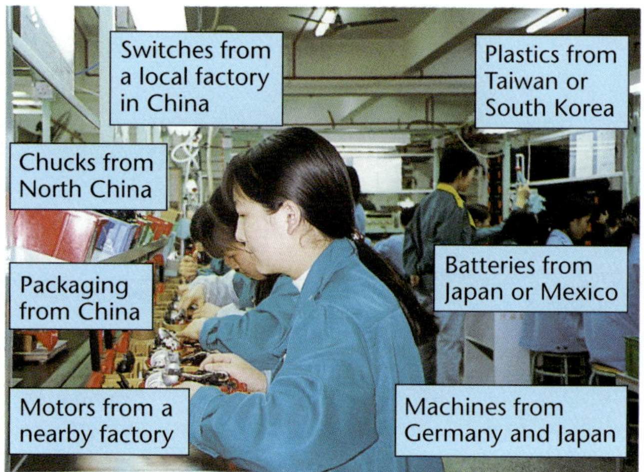

A The inputs – an example of globalisation

C Employers and employees are winners

Advantages for BDCI

- Workers are paid US$12 a week (compared to over $200 a week in USA).
- Other overheads and infrastructure costs are low.
- All imports and exports are duty free.
- Sample products can be produced quickly and at 20% of the cost in Europe.

Advantages for the workers

- Wages are three times what workers would get at home in north China.
- Workers get dormitory accommodation, canteen, sports, health and social facilities provided free.
- Within three years workers can save enough money to buy a house or shop back home.

The processes

The factory is divided into about 40 manufacturing cells where assembly of the different products is carried out, followed by quality control and distribution. The company also has design facilities and a reliability test centre.

The outputs

BDCI produce a range of cordless power tools, mainly drills and screwdrivers. These are sold all over the world, but mainly in the USA and Europe.

The workforce

The factory employs 2000 workers, mostly aged around 18 – 20 and 85% of them female. The workers are brought in from the north of China because local people have become too well off to work for the wages offered (see pages 16 and 17). Workers usually choose to work around 60 hours a week, rather than the standard 44 hours, to earn as much money as possible. The management is made up mostly of Hong Kong Chinese or 'westerners' and the Head Office of the company is still located in Hong Kong. Although Hong Kong costs are ten times as high, the necessary skills and **infrastructure** are still not thought to be well enough developed to locate fully in China.

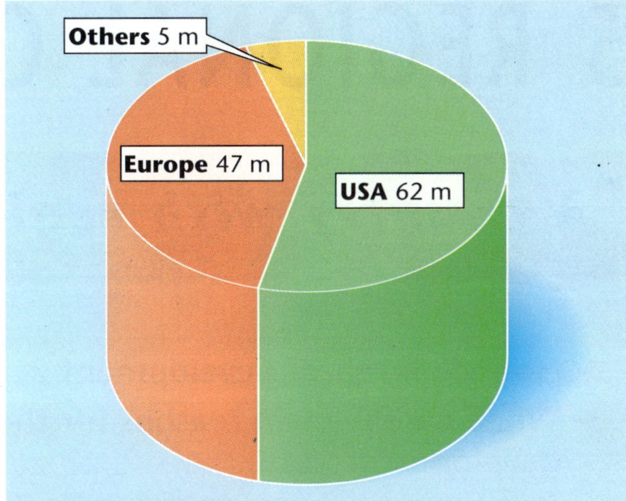

D 1998 Black and Decker sales profile, $millions

The competition

The company has developed a fully integrated plant at Shajing in order to reduce production costs even further. The factory is not only competing with rival companies, but also with other Black and Decker plants around the world. Output from Shajing is growing at a rate of 50% a year at present, and it has taken over work from factories in the UK and North America. The cost advantages make this site an ideal place for manufacturing industry. Many other foreign companies such as Sanyo and Panasonic are found in the same locality. It is almost impossible for the high-cost economies of the west to compete in labour-intensive industries such as this.

FACT FILE

Chinese inventions

The Chinese have a long history as a creative and inventive people. Gas lamps were in use in Chinese homes 2 000 years before those in Europe. Natural gas was found when salt was being obtained from brine water in the ground. The gas was fed through bamboo pipes and burned to evaporate the water to leave salt.

Two geographical inventions of the Chinese were the compass and the seismograph. Knowing directions was very important in traditional towns, because doors and graves were constructed to face south. Early compasses were made of a fish- or a spoon-shaped magnetic stone, which pointed south. The first seismograph was a bronze instrument, with a central column within an outer casing. The column was connected to eight dragons' heads around the casing, each with a ball in its mouth. When an earthquake occurred, one ball fell into the mouth of a frog beneath it, indicating the direction of the quake.

The oldest known piece of writing paper was found in a 2 000-year-old Chinese tomb. Early paper was made from plant materials such as hemp, mulberry bark, straw and seaweed and was more often used as a material for items like hats, jackets and blankets than for writing on.

China was also the birthplace of many other processes, materials and machines, such as block printing, bronze, silk, kites, the crossbow and gunpowder.

5 REGIONAL CONTRASTS

A country with regional inequalities

- How do levels of development vary within China?
- What are the main reasons for the regional differences in development?

Like many countries, China has marked contrasts in the levels of development between its regions. One way to help explain differences in development between regions is to use the idea of core and periphery.

A A village in Shaanxi Province

Core regions are those where there is a great deal of economic activity, such as industry and finance; most of a country's wealth is concentrated here. In China, the core regions are on the coast in provinces such as Guangdong.

Away from the cores there are less wealthy areas: the periphery. Here there is less economic activity and standards of living are lower. In China the periphery is in the centre and west of the country, in provinces such as Shaanxi.

As in other countries, China's core regions have grown at the expense of the periphery. For example, many of the more enterprising workers have left the interior for the coastal areas. This has created a number of social difficulties within the country. Some people believe that if the regional inequalities within China become greater, the country's political stability might be threatened.

B Guangzhou, Guangdong Province

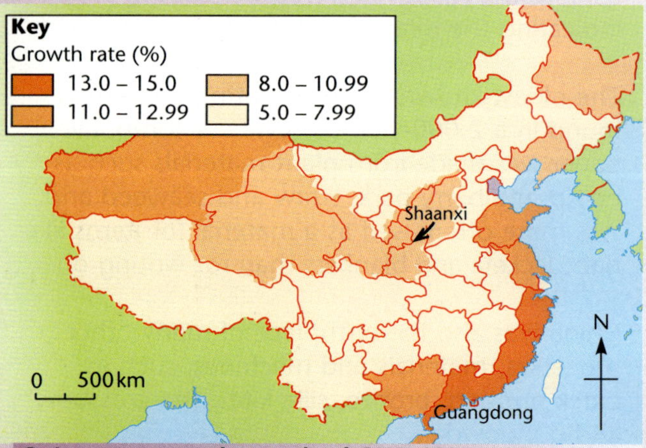

C Average annual growth of GNP, 1985 – 97

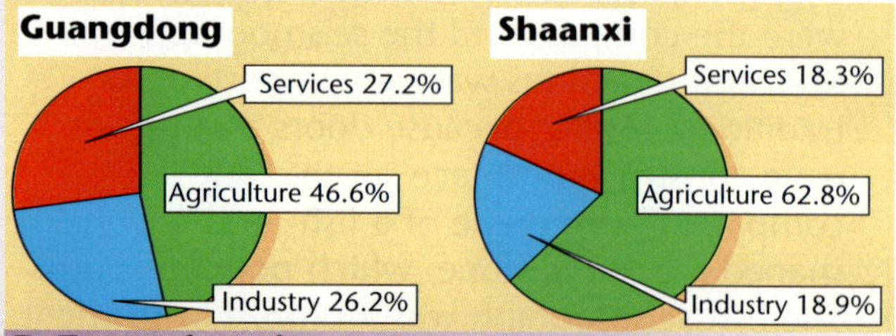

D Types of employment

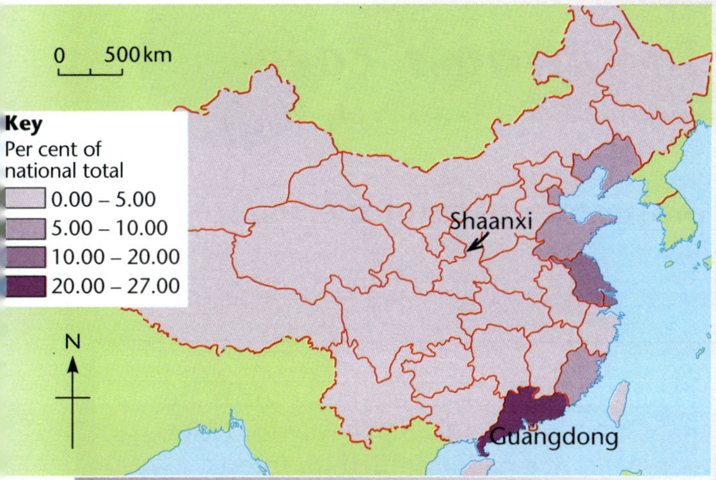

E Foreign capital investment, 1997

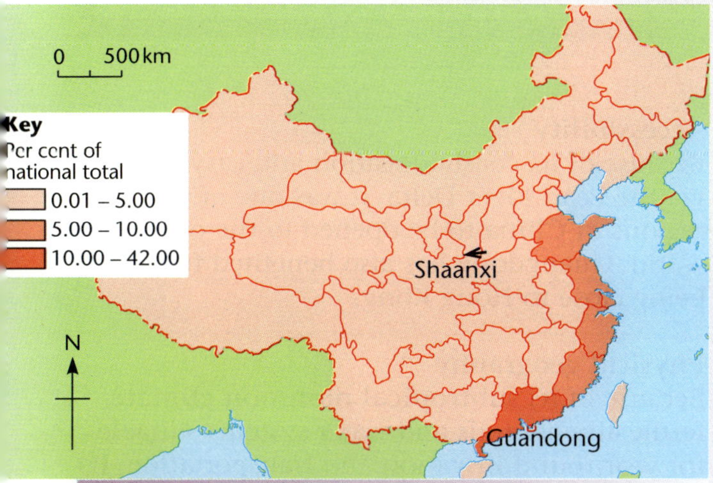

F Exports from China's provinces, 1997

	Guangdong	Shaanxi
Area (km^2)	178 000	205 500
Population 1992 (m)	65.25	34.05
% urban 1991	29.79	24.6

G Key facts

	Guangdong	Shaanxi
Average annual wage (Rmb)	4 027	2434
For agricultural workers	2 730	2095
For industrial workers	4 178	2441

H Average annual wage, 1992

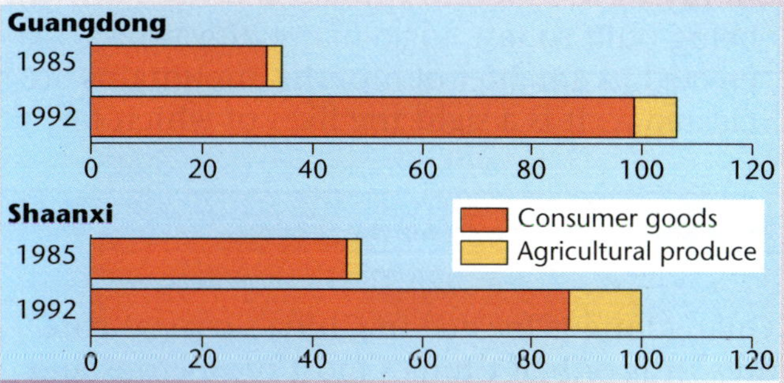

I Total value of retail sales

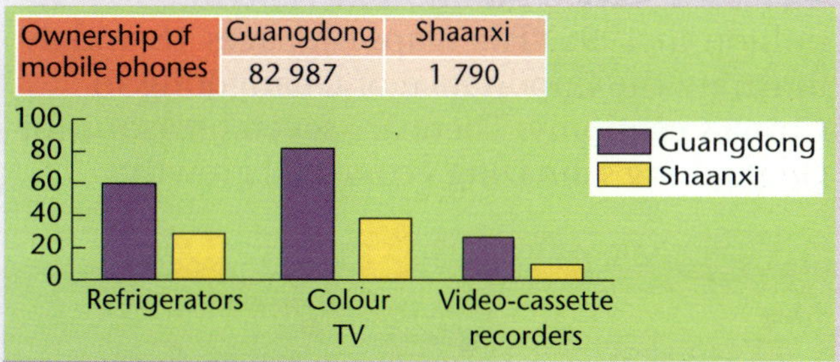

J Ownership of consumer goods per 100 households

FACT FILE

China's richest and poorest regions, 1997

Richest

Region	Gross Domestic Product (100 million Yuan)
Guangdong	7 315
Jiangsu	6 680
Shandong	6 650
Zhejiang	4 638
Henan	4 079
Hebei	3 953

Poorest

Region	Gross Domestic Product (100 million Yuan)
Tibet	76
Qinghai	202
Ningxia	210
Hainan	409
Gansu	781
Guizhou	792

Differences in birth rates within China's regions, 1997

Lowest

Region	Birth Rate (%)
Shanghai	5.50
Beijing	7.91
Tianjin	9.98
Shandong	11.28
Zhejiang	11.41
Jiangsu	11.43

Highest

Region	Birth Rate (%)
Tibet	23.90
Guizhou	22.15
Qinghai	21.80
Yunnan	20.82
Xinjiang	19.66
Hainan	19.18

Guangdong Province in China's core

- Why is Guangdong one of the most prosperous parts of the country?
- How might it develop in the future?

> In my travels around China's southern provinces of Guangdong, I discovered that roads are being built so fast, in so many directions, that no maps are accurate. To make way for cities erected in a matter of months, mountains are being moved, rice paddies filled in, forests cleared … It is a sight the likes of which few people alive today have seen.

Paul Theroux, *Going to See the Dragon*

Guangdong is located in China's coastal core area. It is one of China's most prosperous and heavily populated provinces. Its population increased from 54 million in 1986 to 68 million in 1995. The maps on pages 48 and 49 illustrate the importance of Guangdong in China's economy. There are several reasons for Guangdong's amazing economic growth:

A Guangdong within China's core

B A future megalopolis?

Accessibility
Because of its coastal location and easy access via the Pearl River Delta, it was one of the first regions of China to be opened to the outside world. Guangdong has also benefited from being close to Hong Kong.

Physical geography
Because of its **subtropical monsoon climate**, fertile alluvial soils and water systems suitable for year-round irrigation and transportation, it is a major agricultural region (see pages 6 – 9).

Political and economic factors
Since 1979 the province has benefited from the Chinese government's decisions to encourage trade and investment in some parts of the country's core area.

C Central Shenzhen

Because of its prosperity Guangdong has become a magnet for China's migrant population. Pages 16 and 17 explain the advantages and disadvantages of this migration.

In 1979, the Chinese government created four small areas along its coast as Special Economic Zones (SEZs). Since 1984, 288 'open cities' have been established, mainly along the coast. Firms locating here are given cost and tax incentives. Guangdong Province has three SEZs and one open city. These areas are open to the rest of the world for trade and investment.

Shenzhen SEZ, in Guangdong, on the border of the Hong Kong Special Administrative Region, is 327 km^2 in size. In 1979 it was a small market town of 30 000 people and had 1 500 factories. In 1995 its population was 1.4 million, with 25 000 factories.

Most of the factories are owned by Hong Kong businesses (see pages 46 and 47). The owners do not pay customs duties on goods. Mainland Chinese people are employed in jobs needing large amounts of labour. Highly skilled work is still done in Hong Kong.

Average costs (1997)

	Shenzhen Special Economic Zone	Hong Kong Special Administrative Region
Monthly wages (manufacturing industry)	US$150	US$1 420
Factory premises selling price/m^2	US$200	US$3 878
Office premises monthly rental/m^2	US$10	US$73
High rise flats (selling price/m^2)	US$900	US$11 368
Cost of electricity (per kwh)	US$0.07	US$0.11
Number of foreign firms	14 500	4 943

D Shenzhen's economic advantages

"By 2010 Macau, Shenzhen, Zhuhai and Hong Kong will have developed into a southern China 'megalopolis' with a population of 12 million. The development of science and technology based industries and improved transport links will make this one of the most prosperous urban areas in the world.

Many Hong Kong people will live in Shenzhen and travel to work in Hong Kong. Other areas of China's core will become **megalopolises**, for example the area between Beijing and Tianjin."

E A Shenzhen town planner

FACT FILE

China's prosperous province

In 1996 Guangdong province attracted 40% of the overseas investment made in China. In the same year it accounted for nearly 40% of the country's exports and 30% of its imports. Most exports were textiles and mechanical and electrical products, most imports were primary products and electronics.

The province is now benefitting from a number of improvements in transportation: for example the development of a a new deepwater port at Gaolan in Zhuhai, the opening of the Beijing – Hong Kong railway and the construction of the new airports in Hong Kong and Macau.

Not all of Guangdong is prosperous. Parts of the north and west of Guangdong remain no richer then its far poorer neighbours Guangxi (to the west) and Hunan and Jiangxi (to the north).

However, lower wages in Guangdong's mountainous, less prosperous areas might encourage more firms to locate here in the future. In 1996 the average income of peasants in these areas was only 40% of the average for the province as a whole.

Guangdong's economic growth in recent years has been so fast that the province now has a shortage of labour in some areas. This is a very sharp contrast with the rest of China.

Shaanxi Province in China's periphery

- Why are there poverty-stricken areas in provinces such as Shaanxi?
- How can these levels of poverty be reduced?

Shaanxi Province, in the middle west of China, is part of the country's periphery. Its provincial capital is Xi'an, the former capital of China. More than 80% of Shaanxi consists of mountains and hills. The climate is continental monsoon. The province's gross national product is approximately one third below the average for the country as a whole. Shaanxi's population of 34 million contains 6% of China's most poverty-stricken rural people. The Ankang region, in the Province's Qinba Mountains, is one of its most deprived areas.

SOME CHARACTERISTICS OF THE ANKANG REGION'S POPULATION

- Half the boys and nearly all the girls do not attend school.
- Illiteracy rates are very high.
- **Infant mortality rates** are between 15 and 20% (more than 50% above the national average).
- Many people have severe vitamin deficiencies.
- Maternal mortality rates are 0.5% (100% above the national average).
- There is a high incidence of tuberculosis.
- Roughly half the children are partly stunted in growth because of malnutrition.
- 90% of the children suffer chronic intestinal worm infection.
- Average annual income is 530 yuan (£37).

Why the region's poverty level is high

- The area is mountainous which means that there is very little agricultural land.
- It is difficult for the population to earn sufficient income from cash crops so there is severe underemployment.
- Unlike some rural areas of China, migration to the cities for work is very restricted.
- The area is isolated and there is a serious shortage of both roads and vehicles.
- The population lacks information about job prospects in other parts of the country.
- Individuals have insufficient knowledge and skills to obtain employment.
- They have no spare income to enable them to leave in search of jobs.

A A village in the Qinba Mountains

B Location map of Shaanxi Province

Reducing poverty in Shaanxi

The Chinese government, with the help of funding from the World Bank, has introduced a major welfare project in the Qinba Mountain area. This initiative should benefit the population of the Ankang region.

The project's aims are:

- to reduce poverty by increasing incomes and productivity;
- to improve health and education;
- to reverse the environmental destruction of the upland areas by increasing afforestation;
- to encourage local communities to be involved in decision-making which affects their future.

Other parts of China's periphery with the poorest populations, earning less than 500 yuan per year, include ethnic minority regions in remote **autonomous regions** such as Guangxi, Zhuang, Tibet, Ningxia, Hui and Inner Mongolia. The Chinese government needs to attract more foreign capital to tackle this major problem.

Period	Decrease	Annual average decrease
1978 – 85	250 million to 125 million	17.86 million
1985 – 95	125 million to 65 million	6 million

C Decrease in China's poverty-stricken rural population

Category	% of project funding allocated
Improvements in upland agriculture, e.g. by increasing crop yields on the small amounts of flat land available and creating terraces to improve water and soil conservation	54
Increasing off-farm employment, e.g. by increasing rural labour mobility, providing vocational training, introducing a computerised system for job searching and supporting new rural enterprises such as handicraft industries	30
Improvements in services, e.g. by building health clinics and primary schools, introducing irrigation and rural electrification schemes	11
Developing research and monitoring to ensure that the population in the Ankang region benefits from the Project	4
Providing financial credit for local people to develop co-operative and individual schemes	1

D Main categories of Project funding

FACT FILE

The road to economic recovery

The World Bank is also funding projects to improve Shaanxi's road network. This is supporting the province's 'Master plan for the Poor Areas', which aims to provide year-round access to all the poor townships and to 80% of the villages in Shaanxhi by 2000.

New all-weather roads are helping to increase the mobility of the population by lowering transport costs and reducing travel times. Access to schools and health facilities is gradually improving.

Xi'an is now also one of China's main destinations for tourists. It was once the country's capital and one of the greatest cities in the world, rivalling Rome and Constantinople. Xi'an became a modern tourist attraction after 1974 when a peasant farmer discovered thousands of terracotta soldiers in a field 30km east of the city centre. These were in the tomb of Qin Shihuang, the first emperor of unified China and are on display in the Terracotta Warriors' Museum near Xi'an.

The future prosperity of Shaanxi Province as a whole will depend very much on investment from overseas companies. The trend is encouraging: for example in 1997 overseas investment in the province increased by 81%.

6 CHINA'S FUTURE

Trade and globalization

▶ How is China's role in the world changing?

It's a small world

Developments such as cable television, the Internet, mobile telephones and cheap air travel seem to have drawn different peoples closer together. European firms frequently use Asian companies to carry out their computer programming. Canadian books may be printed in Hong Kong. Coca Cola and BMW cars can be seen in cities of every continent. This is often a result of the process of **globalization**.

The money pours in

Around 85% of the investment in China is from overseas Chinese who have made their fortunes in places such as Hong Kong, Singapore, Malaysia or Taiwan. In the past these investments were not allowed, but nowadays China has a more open market economy. US trans-national companies, like General Motors and IBM, have contributed more than US$5 billion of the remaining investment.

Year	1981	1986	1991	1996
Primary goods	10.2	11.3	16.1	21.9
Manufactured goods	11.8	19.7	55.7	129.1

A Changing Chinese exports ($US billions)

Changing trade

China is undergoing rapid economic growth and is becoming a major player in the world economic community. In 1978 China was the country ranked 32nd in world trade but by 1996 it had risen to eighth. Many people forecast that its GNP will overtake that of the USA by 2015.

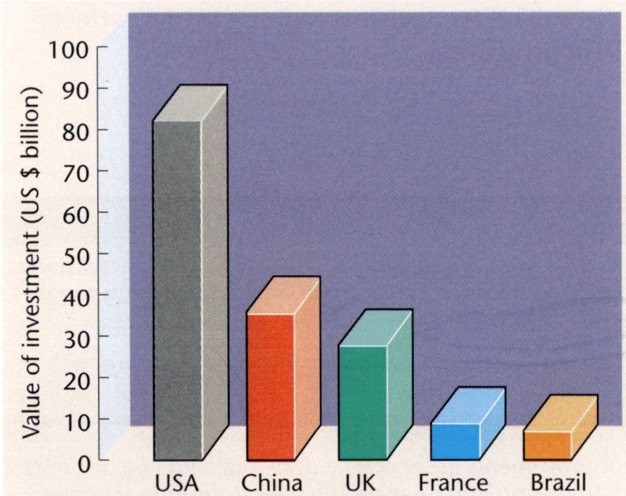

B The top five receivers of foreign investment in 1997

You may not be surprised that clothing and toys are China's top two exports (50% of all toys sold in the world are made in China), but would you know that telecommunications equipment is China's third highest export?

Some of China's advantages

China has the largest home market in the world and one of the fastest growing economies in the world. It also has the most widely spoken first language. It is a member of the Asia-Pacific Economic Co-operation group (APEC), which includes the USA and Japan. APEC accounts for 46% of global trade.

The next 20 years?

The World Bank has made two different predictions for China in the next 20 years. If the present reforms fail then they forecast it will remain a low-income and unequal society, full of possible conflicts. If China succeeds, it will become a middle-income country, with earnings similar to Portugal, South Korea or Argentina. Hundreds of millions of people will be directly affected by the outcome.

C Most widely spoken first languages (% of world population)

%	Language
15.2	Mandarin
5.5	English
4.6	Spanish
3.2	Bengali
3.1	Hindi
2.9	Portuguese
2.9	Russian

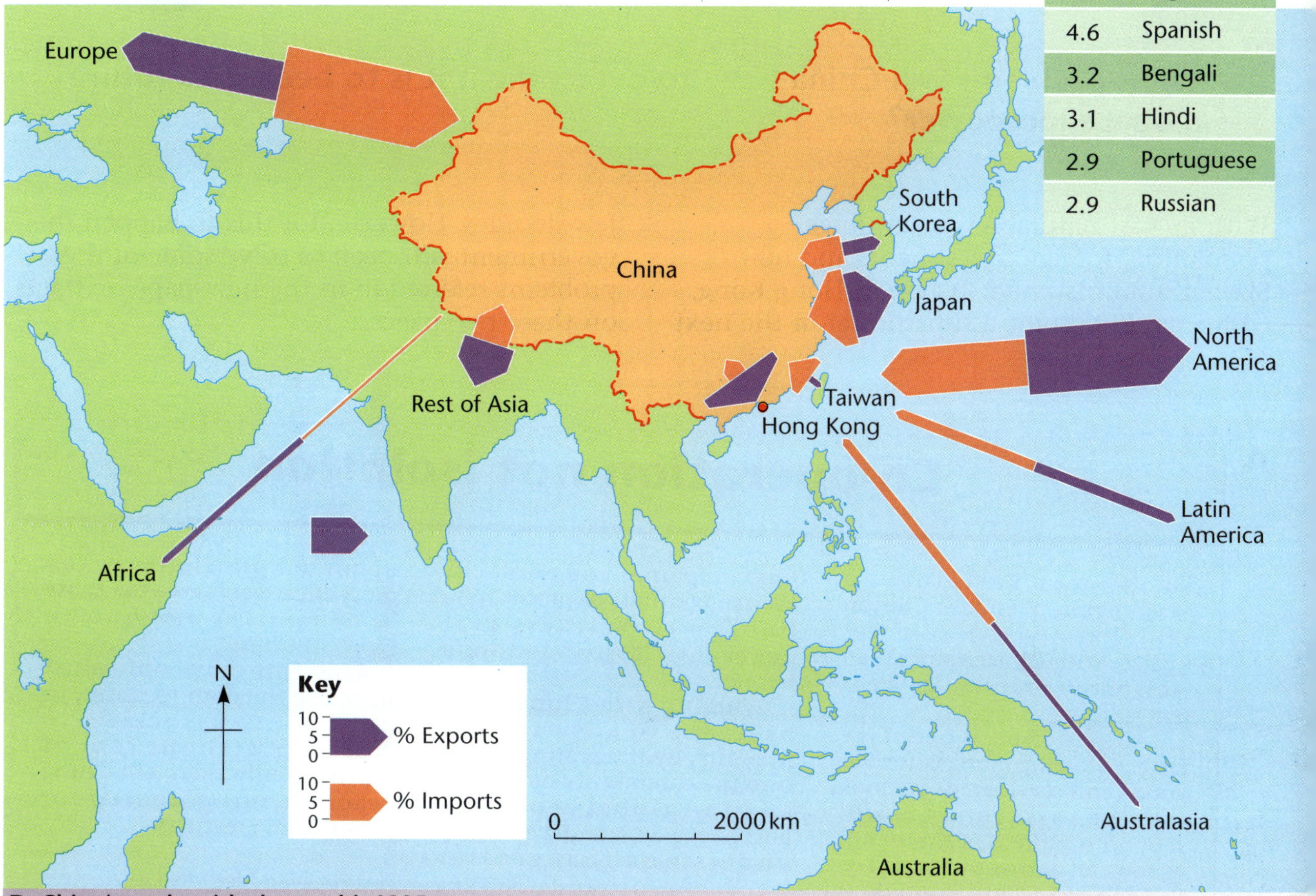

D China's trade with the world, 1995

FACT FILE

An opening market

The industrialised countries of North America, Europe and Japan are very keen to increase their trade with China. Even though these countries may lose out as China can produce labour-intensive manufactured goods more cheaply, they can still sell them their hi-tech products, services and even primary products such as grain. Japan is, perhaps, in the best position to gain, as it is located close to the emerging giant.

Many less economically developed countries of Asia also see greater trade with China as good for their economies. The growing economy of China will have to import far more in the future. Many people in these countries also believe that wage rises in China will soon make their own products more competitive (see table below).

Country	Unskilled workers	Skilled workers
China	240	100
Indonesia	200	55
Philippines	175	85
Taiwan	150	50
India	100	52
Japan	70	5

Percentage growth in wages forecast from 1992 to 2020 (World Bank estimates).

China's challenges

▶ **What problems will China have to overcome if it is to become a future global superpower?**

With its vast natural resources, huge population, foreign investments and new Special Administrative Region of Hong Kong, China could become a superpower in the next few decades. However, for this to happen the government will need to solve some of the problems referred to in the newspaper extracts on these two pages.

A

Co-operation not isolation

In a speech yesterday in Washington, President Clinton said that America must co-operate with China, rather than isolate the country. He went on:

"Already China is one of the fastest growing markets for our goods and services. As we look into the next century, it will support hundreds of thousands of jobs all across our country. But access to China's markets remains restricted for many of our companies and products. We can continue to press China to open its markets as it engages in major economic reform.

Working with China is the best way to advance our interests. By integrating China into the community of nations and the global economy, helping its leadership understand that greater freedom profoundly serves China's interests, and standing up for our principles, we can most effectively serve the cause of democracy and human rights in China.

The Chinese people must have the freedom to speak, to publish, to associate, to worship without fear of reprisal. Only then will China reach its full potential for growth and greatness."

South China Morning Post, 24 June 1998

B

China's rural problems

Protesting workers, rioting peasants and Sunday's bomb explosion in Changsha, the capital of Hunan province, add up to a scary picture of just how bad things are in parts of China. In Mao Zedong's home province, the economic problems are increasing so fast that unrest can easily turn into revolt.

Last year angry workers staged 60 protests outside the provincial party headquarters, so many that the authorities issued an emergency decree on December 29 outlawing further protests. Yet the protests are continuing in this rural province of 60 million. In Changde city, a third of its 10 000 cotton mill factory workers have been laid off without pay, and on Monday, 500 blocked a new highway to press demands for three months' **subsistence wages**. In November, 200 workers from the Laiteer Company blocked traffic in Changsha holding up banners which said: "Not a yuan in six months, we want rice to eat".

Hunan's industrial economy is close to breakdown and the government is bankrupt. From an industrial workforce of four million in **state-owned enterprises** (SOEs), a million have already been fired. The province has 140 SOEs in operation which are losing money, especially in the textile sector. The central government is trying to reduce over-production and return the sector to profitability. Last year it fired 0.5 million textile workers. This year the target is 1.1 million workers. Hunan laid off 21 000 workers last year but the big push was supposed to come this year. "We just can't do it now, it will undermine social stability," a spokesman at the Industrial Management Centre of the Hunan Textile Bureau admitted. "The government is in financial difficulties so it cannot even support the workers already laid off."

South China Morning Post, 23 January 1999

C

Fastest growing economy in the world has fastest growing pollution problem

Just as in the United states in the 1950s, everybody wants a refrigerator in today's emerging consumer society in China. In 1984, only 3 per cent of the households in Beijing owned a fridge. By 1989 this had risen to 60 per cent. The problem is that all these fridges use chlorofluorocarbons as coolant.

Carbon dioxide is the most abundant of greenhouse gases, but pound for pound CFCs are hundreds of times more effective in trapping heat and are extremely persistent.

What remains of China's wildlife is also under threat because of the nation's economic success. The rain forests of the south have all but disappeared, while in the north-west, logging is rapidly reducing swathes of primary conifer forests. Also, climate change might well affect the flora and fauna that inhabit the mountains on the eastern edge of the Tibetan plateau.

Best known and best loved of all the inhabitants of these mountains is the giant panda. Already the panda is one of the world's most seriously endangered animals, and the focus of intense international concern.

Sunday Standard, 11 July 1993

D

China: a country with inequalities

Gogglebox

Villagers in the remote Simao district of Yunnan province watch television for the first time after authorities fixed up a satellite dish.

Life on the footbridge

A migrant couple from Yunnan living on a footbridge overlooking Shanghai's prosperous Bund district.

In 1997, the GNP for Shanghai was 7 954 Rmb per year; for Yunnan it was 1 332 Rmb per year.

FACT FILE

Regions in China with the highest number of pollution accidents, 1997

REGION	Number of pollution accidents	Types of pollution accidents				
		Water Pollution	Air Pollution	Solid Wastes Pollution	Noise and Vibration Pollution	Other types
Guangxi	374	141	170	12	43	8
Zhejiang	169	109	50	5	0	5
Shandong	141	38	43	10	3	45
Guangdong	139	95	33	1	10	0
Jiangxi	128	67	57	1	3	0
Liaoning	112	8	82	4	4	14
Gansu	110	59	26	7	18	0
Totals for China as a whole	1 992	986	752	55	119	80

ISSUE 1: can the Chinese government overcome the difficulties caused by the country's ethnic diversity?

About 93% of the population of China is Han Chinese. Approximately 7% of the population consists of 55 different minority nationalities. Examples of the largest minorities are listed in table **A**. Mao Zedong once said:

"China has a vast territory, abundant resources and a large population. Of these three, the Han population possess one, namely, they are many in number; the minority population possesses two, they have vast territories and resources".

Newspaper extract B illustrates how the presence of **ethnic minorities** in China can cause problems for the Government.

A Examples of China's ethnic minorities

Minority	Population	Areas of distribution
Zhuang	13 378 162	Guangxi, Yunnan, Guangdong, Guizhou
Uighurs	6 019 632	Xinjiang, Hunan
Tibetans	3 970 068	Tibet, Sichuan, Qinghai, Gansu, Yunnan
Mongolians	3 411 657	Inner Mongolia, Xinjiang, Liaoning, Jilin, Heilongjiang, Qinghai, Hebei, Yunnan Henan, Gansu

ISSUE 2: will China be able to feed its population?

Two thirds of China is taken up with mountains and deserts. Only 10% of the land is available for cultivation. At its current rate of growth, the Chinese population will reach 1.5 billion by 2015, having trebled in less than ten years. The amount of arable land is reducing and the growth rate in grain production has begun to slow down.

B Glimpse of a troubled land

XINJIANG IN TROUBLE

Bit by bit, a picture is emerging of China's most troubled region, Xinjiang, in the far north-west. For the past year or two, occasional guarded reports in official Chinese newspapers have suggested the existence of separatist movements in the region. Amnesty International has put together the most comprehensive account so far of the persecution of the region's ethnic majority, the Uighurs.

According to Amnesty, Xinjiang is the only region of China where political prisoners are known to have been executed in recent years. The Uighurs are Muslims, so, as in Buddhist Tibet, there is a religious divide between the ethnic locals and the Han Chinese. Many Chinese have migrated to Xinjiang, as they have to Tibet. The Uighurs fear that their culture is being destroyed, and that they will eventually become a minority in their own region. Culture and religion foster the Uighurs' longings for independence. Xinjiang is mostly a desert three times the size of France, but under the ground are oil and other minerals, prizes that drew the Chinese – and keep them there.

The Economist, May 1999

ISSUE 3: can the Chinese government convince western countries that it has an improving human rights record?

Many people in western countries feel that China has a poor record on human rights. They point out the events in Tiananmen Square in Beijing on the night of 4 June 1989 when the Chinese Government ordered its army to fire on protesting students, which resulted in large numbers of deaths. But many Chinese feel that the west has failed to acknowledge what they believe to be their government's improving record on **human rights.**

This is an important issue because the USA in particular wishes to see this improvement before giving China any more concessions for trading with western countries.

ISSUE 4: can the country reduce the inequalities in its regional economic growth?

There are marked contrasts in prosperity between China's provinces as illustrated on pages 48 and 49. There is a growing gap in living standards between rural and urban China: the agricultural economy is growing at about 3% per annum and the urban economy at more that 20%. The gap is widening each year. This is one of the reasons why some people try to leave China illegally. See extract C, map D and photograph E.

D Location map of Tantou village

A nightmare month-long journey in an overcrowded tugboat followed by 19 days behind bars in Australia and 11 days in a re-education camp back home have done nothing to dampen Xiao Zhang's spirits "I want to go back to Australia with my whole family. I will try again," the 23-year-old insisted over lunch in his village in Tantou, China. The Tantou area, in Fujian province, is infamous for its illegal immigrants who cross the Pacific Ocean in freighters and rickety fishing boats.

The village of Tantou is a long way from the nice New South Wales beach he and 58 fellow passengers strolled onto last month, changing into suits and seeking a new life. But it is not nearly as poor as many other Chinese villages: illegal immigrants who have fled for Australia, the United States and Europe send back thousands of yuan every month. There is a local saying here: "To find gold, sneak out by boat. One goes, whole family wins gold".

Extract from *South China Morning Post* 23 May 1999

C Risking all for a land of gold

E Tantou village

FACT FILE

Some changes in the Chinese people's lives 1985-97

ITEM	1985	1990	1995	1996	1997
Income earned (Yuan)					
Average annual income of farmers	397	686	1 577	1 926	2 090
Average annual income of urban workers	1 148	2 140	5 500	6 210	6 470
Income spent (Yuan)					
Average annual expenditure by farmers	347	571	1 479	1 816	1 930
Average annual expenditure by urban workers	802	1 686	5 044	5 634	6 048
Culture					
TV sets per 100 households	11.7	44.4	80.7	88.0	92.4
Newspapers per 100 persons per day	5.21	3.87	4.07	4.04	4.30
Number of books published	45 603	80 224	101 381	112 813	120 888
Education					
Number of graduates from institutions of higher education (per 10 000 persons)	31.6	61.4	80.5	83.9	82.9
Health					
Doctors per 10 000 persons	13.3	15.4	15.8	15.9	16.1

Statistics

	UK	CHINA	AUSTRALIA	SOUTH AFRICA	USA
Total area (km^2)	244 880	9 596 960	7 686 850	1 221 040	9 809 431
Total population (millions)	58.3	1 210.0	18.4	44.0	263.6
Population density: people per km^2	243	130	2	35	28

Population

	UK	CHINA	AUSTRALIA	SOUTH AFRICA	USA
Birth rate (per 1 000) people	13	17	14	27	15
Death rate (per 1 000) people	11	7	7	12	9
Life expectancy (male and female)	74M 79F	69M 72F	77M 83F	54M 58F	73M 79F
Fertility (children per female)	2	2	2	4	2
Population structure: 0–14 15–59 60+	19% 61% 21%	27% 65% 9%	22% 63% 15%	37% 57% 6%	21% 62% 17%
Urban population	90%	29%	86%	57%	77%

Environment and economy

	UK	CHINA	AUSTRALIA	SOUTH AFRICA	USA
Rate of urban growth per year	0.3%	4.3%	1.4%	3.0%	1.3%
Land use (%): arable grass forest	27 46 10	10 43 14	7% 54% 14%	10 67 4	19 25 30
% workforce in: farming industry services	2 28 70	73 14 13	6% 24% 70%	13 25 62	3 25 72
GNP per person (US$)	$18 700	$620	$18 720	$3 160	$26 980
Unemployment	8.3%	2.8%	8.5%	45%	5.6%
Energy used (tonnes/person/year)	5.40	0.35	7.38	2.49	10.74

Society and quality of life

	UK	CHINA	AUSTRALIA	SOUTH AFRICA	USA
Infant mortality (deaths per 1000 births)	6	38	5	5.4	7
People per doctor	300	1000	400	1 750	420
Food supply (calories per person per day)	3 317	2 727	3 179	2 695	3 732
Adult literacy	99%	70%	99%	81%	99%
TVs per 1000 people	434	31	666	98	814
Aid received or given per person	$53 given	$3 received	$62 given	$10 received	$33 given
Spending on education (as % of GNP)	5.3	2.4	5.5	3.8	7.0
Spending on military (as % of GNP)	4.0	3.7	2.4	3.0	5.3
United Nations Human Development Index (out of 1.0)	0.92	0.59	0.93	0.71	0.94

Figures are for 1992–97. Source: *Philip's Geographical Digest* (United Nations, World Bank). The Human Development Index is worked out by the UN. It is a summary of national income, life expectancy, adult literacy and education. It is a measure of human progress. In 1992, the HDI ranged from 0.21 to 0.94.

General

Longest river: River Yangtze River (6 300km)
Highest mountain: Mount Qomolangma, China and Nepal (8 848m)
Currency: Renmimbi yuan
Capital: Beijing
Government: Single-party Communist Republic
Religion: Buddhism, Taoism, Islam. More than half the people say they are atheists.
Languages: Mandarin Chinese (official)

Social

Health Care Institutions

	1992	1993	1994	1995	1996
Hospitals	61352	60784	67857	67807	67964
Hospitalls at and above county level	13917	14713	14762	14771	15056
Sanatorium	639	600	587	582	528
Clinics	125873	115161	105984	104406	103472
Specialized stations	1845	1872	1905	1895	1887
Sanitation and disease control stations	3673	3609	3611	3629	4000
Maternity and child care centres	2841	2791	2857	2832	2764
Total	204787	193586	191742	190057	188803

Student population

	Million people					
	1992	1993	1994	1995	1996	1997
Colleges	2.184	2.536	2.799	2.906	3.02	3.17
Specialized secondary schools	2.408	2.82	3.198	3.722	4.228	4.654
High schools	47.708	47.391	49.817	53.71	57.397	60.179
Primary schools	122.013	124.212	128.226	131.95	136.15	139.95

Living space

Per capita living floor space (sq m)	1995	1996	1997
Rural areas	21	21.7	22.5
Urban areas	8	8.4	8,8

Economic

Import and exports (US$ billion)

Items	Total	Exports	Imports
1992	165.53	84.94	80.59
1993	195.7	91.74	103.96
1994	236.73	121.04	115.69
1995	280.85	148.77	132.08
1996	289.9	151.1	138.8
1997	325.06	182.7	142.36

Major farm crops

Crop (1,000 tonnes)	1993	1994	1995	1996
Grain	456488	445101	466618	504535
Cereal	405174	393891	416116	451271
Rice	177702	175933	185226	195103
Wheat	106390	99297	102207	110569
Corn	102704	99275	111986	127471
Soybeans	15310	16000	13500	13220
Oil bearing crops	18039	19896	22503	22106
Peanuts	8421	9682	10235	10138
Rapeseed	6939	7492	9777	9201
Cotton	3739	4341	4768	4203
Tea	599941	588468	588553	593386
Apple	9069557	11129017	14007662	17047250
Citrus	6560974	6805445	8224984	8456587
Banana	2700680	2897832	3125003	2535591

Trade with other countries

Country	Japan	Malaysia	Taiwan	Russia	United Kingdom	Canada	United States	Brazil	Egypt	South Africa
1995										
Total	57467	3346	17882	5463	4764	4214	40830	1991	453	1322
Exports	28463	1281	3098	1665	2792	1536	24711	759	440	633
Imports	29005	2065	14784	3799	1972	2681	16118	1232	13	688
1996										
Total	339059	1614	18984	6846	5082	4186	42841	2248	408	1347
Exports	30875	1371	2803	1693	3201	1616	26685	763	405	683
Imports	29184	2243	16182	5153	1551	2570	16155	1484	3	664

Glossary

accessibility how easy it is to get to a place from other locations

acid rain rain with a pH of less than 5.6 that can be harmful to plants and animals

adult illiteracy rate the percentage of a country's population unable to read.

alluvium any material that has been deposited by rivers, particularly after flooding

arable farming the growing of crops

autonomous region areas of China in which minority peoples have partial self-government. These are Inner Mongolia, Ningxia, Xinjiang, Guangxi and Tibet

birth rate the number of births in a year for every 1 000 people in a place

continental climate a climate which is hot in summer and cold in winter and generally dry. This climate is found inland in large land masses in the mid-latitudes

convectional uplift the rising of warmer, lighter air which then cools. This may result in condensation, cloud formation and rainfall

crust the thin outer layer of the earth, which includes the continents and the ocean floors

death rate the number of deaths in a year for every 1 000 people in a place

desertification the changing of an area so that it turns into a desert.

dykes (or dikes) a mound or embankment built to prevent flooding

epicentre the point on the earth's surface directly above the focus of an earthquake

ethnic minorities a relatively small number of people within a country, considered by the majority of the population to be different because of their ancestry, culture and customs

fault a crack in the rocks, along which movement has taken place

floating workers migrant workers who have left their home area to look for work elsewhere, usually in big cities, but do not have a permanent place to live

focus the place under the ground where an earthquake starts

globalization the increasing spread of common information, ideas and products to all parts of the world

godown a factory warehouse, used mainly for storage

greenhouse effect the warming of the atmosphere as it absorbs some of the heat given off by the earth. This may be increasing as we put more gases like CO_2 into the air

Gross National Product (GNP) a measure of the wealth created by a country's business both at home and abroad

growing season the length of time during a year when it is warm enough and wet enough for plants to grow

Hong Kong Special Administrative Region on 1 July, 1997, Hong Kong became a special administrative region within China. It will have this status until 30 June 2047

human rights the basic rights that any person in the world should be able to claim

hydro-electric power energy produced by using the power of running water to turn generators

incentive an encouragement or reward given for doing something

infanticide the killing of children with the consent of a parent

infant mortality rate the percentage of children dying in childbirth.

infrastructure the range of communications and other services, such as roads, electricity and water supply, that is needed for economic development to take place

international migration the permanent or semi-permanent movement of people from one country to another

irrigation artificially adding water to farmland to grow crops

joint venture company a business partnership involving Chinese and foreign companies

Karst scenery the name comes from the Karst region of Slovenia but is now given to any area of limestone which contains, for example, underground streams, caves and dry valleys

levée a bank of material along the course of a river. This may be naturally formed by the river depositing alluvium when it floods or by people building artificial banks to prevent flooding

life expectancy the age to which a person in a particular place can expect to live

load the material being transported in a stream or river

loess a fine, silty soil. It can be very fertile, but can also be easily eroded if left unprotected

magnitude the size or strength of something, such as an earthquake

manufacturing goods made by hand or with the use of machinery, usually in a factory

market economy an economy where private individuals or companies can carry out their business with little intervention by the government

megalopolis a large urban area with more than ten million inhabitants which combines many individual cities

migrant a person moving from one country to another, or from one region to another, to settle or to work

nullah in Hong Kong, a large drainage channel conveying flood water and sewage into Victoria Harbour

open city the Treaty of Nanking, 1842, allowed five Chinese cities to become 'open' for trade with Western countries. People from the west were allowed to live in these cities, one of which was Shanghai

plateau a large and relatively flat upland area

population density the number of people living in a unit of area, e.g. people per square km^2

population distribution the way in which people are spread out across an area

quotas a limit set on how much should be produced in a given length of time

raw materials products obtained from agriculture, forestry, fishing and mining

respiratory diseases diseases which affect breathing, such as colds, bronchitis and pneumonia

richter scale a scale used to measure the magnitude of earthquakes

river basin an area drained by a river and its tributaries

river plain an area of flat land crossed by a river

satellite town a new town located outside a city, planned as a self-contained community providing work for its inhabitants

seismologist a scientist who studies earthquakes

soil erosion the removal of soil from an area by any combination of methods such as water, wind or gravity

special administrative region on 1 July 1997, Hong Kong became a special administrative region within China. It will have this status until 30 June 2047.

state owned enterprises firms owned by the government.

subsistence wages income received by a person who can provide the bare necessities of life.

subtropical monsoon climate a climate experienced in areas immediately outside the tropics, in which there is a seasonal change in air flows and rainfall. In winter it is dry; in summer there can be heavy rainfall.

superpower a large country with a very big population and great military power. Such countries control or influence many other countries

terraces steps cut into hillsides to provide flat areas of land for farming and control erosion

topsoil the surface layer of a soil, which is usually more fertile

toxic poisonous

tributaries smaller streams or rivers flowing into larger ones

underemployed a person who has not got enough work to earn a subsistence wage

village or ownership enterprise a business not directly agricultural, run within a village or small suburban area, usually operating as part of the market economy

water table the upper surface of water under the ground. The level to which water fills up a hole dug into the ground

weathered broken down by physical, chemical or biological processes

World Bank an international banking organisation which obtains money partly from national governments but also from borrowing. It then loans this money to support aid projects in economically developing countries.

Finding out more about China

Disasters and weather
http://izzy.online.discovery.com

Population
http://www.cpirc.org.cn/eindex.htm

China
http://sun.sino.uni-heidelberg.de/igcs/

Chinese Embassy, Washington
http://www.china-embassy.org/China/China.htm

Chinese Government Internet Information Centre
http://www.chinanews.org/China/indexE.html

CIA Worldfactbook
http://www.odci.gov/cia/publications/factbook/ch.html

The Statistics of China
http://www.umich.edu/~iinet/chinadata/stat/

Maps of China
http://www.chinapage.com/map.html

China Dimensions
http://sedac.ciesin.org/china/

Professional Association for China's Environment
http://www.chinaenvironment.net/

Environmental Protection
http://svr1-pek.unep.net/soechina/index.htm

UN Development Programme data
http://www.undp.org

Unicef data
http://www.unicef.org/sowc98

Index

Bold type refers to terms included in the glossary.
Italic type refers to photographs or maps